Institute of Leadership
& Management

superseries

Communicating
One-to-One
at Work

FIFTH EDITION

Published for the
Institute of Leadership & Management

ELSEVIER

AMSTERDAM • BOSTON • HEIDELBERG • LONDON • NEW YORK • OXFORD
PARIS • SAN DIEGO • SAN FRANCISCO • SINGAPORE • SYDNEY • TOKYO
Pergamon Flexible Learning is an imprint of Elsevier

Pergamon
Flexible
Learning

Pergamon Flexible Learning is an imprint of Elsevier
Linacre House, Jordan Hill, Oxford OX2 8DP, UK
30 Corporate Drive, Suite 400, Burlington, MA 01803, USA

First edition 1986
Second edition 1991
Third edition 1997
Fourth edition 2003
Fifth edition 2007

Editor: David Pardey

Based on material in previous editions of this work

British Library Cataloguing in Publication Data
A catalogue record for this book is available from the British Library

Library of Congress Cataloguing in Publication Data
A catalogue record for this book is available from the Library of Congress

ISBN 978-0-08-046438-1

For information on all Pergamon Flexible Learning publications
visit our website at http://books.elsevier.com

Institute of Leadership & Management
Registered Office
1 Giltspur Street
London
EC1A 9DD
Telephone: 020 7294 2470
www.i-l-m.com
ILM is part of the City & Guilds Group

Typeset by Charon Tec Ltd (A Macmillan Company), Chennai, India
www.charontec.com
Printed and bound in Great Britain

07 08 09 10 11   10 9 8 7 6 5 4 3 2 1

Contents

Contents

Series preface

Whether you are a tutor/trainer or studying management development to further your career, Super Series provides an exciting and flexible resource to help you to achieve your goals. The fifth edition is completely new and up-to-date, and has been structured to perfectly match the Institute of Leadership & Management (ILM)'s new unit-based qualifications for first line managers. It also harmonizes with the 2004 national occupational standards in management and leadership, providing an invaluable resource for S/NVQs at Level 3 in Management.

Super Series is equally valuable for anyone tutoring or studying any management programmes at this level, whether leading to a qualification or not. Individual workbooks also support short programmes, which may be recognized by ILM as Endorsed or Development Awards, or provide the ideal way to undertake CPD activities.

For learners, coping with all the pressures of today's world, Super Series offers you the flexibility to study at your own pace to fit around your professional and other commitments. You don't need a PC or to attend classes at a specific time – choose when and where to study to suit yourself! And you will always have the complete workbook as a quick reference just when you need it.

For tutors/trainers, Super Series provides an invaluable guide to what needs to be covered, and in what depth. It also allows learners who miss occasional sessions to 'catch up' by dipping into the series.

Super Series provides unrivalled support for all those involved in first line management and supervision.

Unit specification

Title:	Communicating one-to-one at work		Unit Ref:	M3.32
Level:	3			
Credit value:	1			

Learning outcomes	Assessment criteria	
The learner will	**The learner can (in an organization with which the learner is familiar)**	
1. Understand the impact of non-verbal communication	1.1	Identify a range of non-verbal behaviours which can affect people in the workplace
2. Understand the importance of one-to-one communication	2.1 2.2 2.3	Explain the importance of one-to-one communication List two methods of direct communication used in the workplace Explain the importance of succinct and accurate records of one-to-one oral communication
3. Know how to conduct interviews in the workplace	3.1 3.2 3.3 3.4	Prepare for and plan an interview for a specific situation in your organization Explain how to conduct interviews effectively, lawfully and ethically Decide what record keeping is required for the type of interview Explain how you would provide feedback to the interviewee where appropriate

Workbook introduction

1 ILM Super Series study links

This workbook addresses the issues of *Communicating One-to-One at Work*. Should you wish to extend your study to other Super Series workbooks covering related or different subject areas, you will find a comprehensive list at the back of this book.

2 Links to ILM qualifications

This workbook relates to the learning outcomes of Unit M3.32 Communicating one-to-one at work from the ILM Level 3 Award, Certificate and Diploma in First Line Management.

3 Workbook objectives

Being an effective communicator is key to the success of any manager. In essence, this means giving and receiving information or messages in a way that avoids any misunderstanding and using the method – or combination of methods – best suited to the situation.

In this workbook we are going to focus on spoken communication, and visual communication in the form of 'body language'. Both are at the heart of meetings between two people, in which information is exchanged for a wide variety of purposes, ranging from ensuring that people have understood instructions, to making decisions and developing relationships.

Whatever the nature of the meeting, there are a number of basic skills that you should always employ, including effective listening and questioning, and being aware of your own body language and that of others.

3.1 Objectives

When you have completed this workbook you will be better able to:

- communicate effectively in one-to-one situations using the most appropriate method;
- understand the power of non-verbal communication and take it into account when you are both sending and receiving information;
- recognize and respond to body language and behaviour;
- conduct interviews effectively and with confidence.

Session A
One-to-one meetings

1 Introduction

Have you ever been in a situation like this?

> One morning Ella came into the office, switched on her computer and proceeded to collect her e-mail messages. She didn't normally receive anything of much importance first thing, so she was rather surprised when an e-mail arrived from Graham, her manager, marked 'personal'. She was even more surprised – in fact, shocked – when she read the e-mail: 'Ella, I'm afraid it's taking far too long for you to complete that project proposal I asked you to draw up next week. I've decided to hand the job over to someone else. You should get on with your normal work this morning.'
>
> Ella almost cried out in dismay. 'I don't believe this,' she thought. 'How could he push me off the project just like that? Why didn't he talk to me first?'

If you have experienced something like this, you'll know only too well that there are many situations in which there is no substitute for a one-to-one meeting. Although other forms of communication have an important role to play in effective management (as we'll discuss later in this session), if you want to deliver a message to someone in an understanding way, and get their reactions and respond accordingly, you need to have a meeting.

2 Types of one-to-one meetings

One-to-one meetings, whether with members of your team or with people outside the team, can be either informal or formal.

Informal meetings with staff can occur on a daily basis. They may arise from a request for information or advice, or because a problem has occurred and a solution needs to be found as a matter of some urgency.

Formal meetings will have been set up in advance. They may take place to discuss some aspect of the project you are working on, if it only concerns the work of one team member, but they are more likely to be for reasons such as the formal tracking of work progress, appraisal or counselling. Some of the types of formal meetings you may encounter are covered later in the session.

3 Setting up meetings

Informal meetings might happen in the corridor, or at the desk of one of the people taking part. Sometimes it might be appropriate to find a quiet, or neutral space, such as a meeting room, or perhaps some comfortable seating in a coffee area. The question, or comment that gives rise to the meeting will probably determine the location that seems most appropriate.

There are two main issues to consider when you are thinking about setting up a meeting that is planned in advance.

- Where will it take place? If you have your own office, should the meeting be held there, or would a neutral space be more appropriate?
- How are you going to invite the person to the meeting?

The place where the meeting is held has an affect on the tone of the meeting, and can give messages to the person you are meeting before any words are spoken. The right physical conditions will also help you to listen properly, and to get the best out of the meeting.

Activity 1 · 3 mins

Imagine you have set up a monthly progress meeting with a member of staff at which you want to discuss various problems that have arisen with their work. What preparations can you make to help ensure that you listen carefully and don't get distracted?

_____

_____

_____

Among the basic preparations you can make are to:

■ book a quiet room where you can meet;
■ make sure the room is comfortable for both of you;
■ ensure there are no interruptions.

The way you choose to ask the other person to attend the meeting can also have an important effect. Sending a memo or an e-mail in which you suggest the time and ask for the other person to confirm, sets a very different tone from just arranging the meeting in person or on the phone.

4 Communicating in one-to-one meetings

When the meeting is underway you need to conduct it in the best way to achieve what you need from it. This involves planning, paying attention to verbal communication and taking account of non-verbal communication.

Activity 2

8 mins

The following description of a one-to-one meeting illustrates how **not** to conduct such a meeting. As you read it, make a note of anything you would avoid doing as the manager in this situation.

Julie manages a small Customer Services team in a large department store. Recently the store has decided to implement a Total Quality Management Programme and she has been on a one-day introductory course where she was asked to look at ways in which her team could improve the service they provide to customers. She holds a team meeting to discuss possible areas for improvement and it is agreed that they would start by looking at the complaints received from customers. The first step is for a member of the team, Anne, to go through the recent files of complaints and sort them into categories.

After a couple of days Anne comes to Julie and asks for a brief meeting to discuss what she should be doing. They sit down at Julie's desk.

Julie: How are you getting on Anne? Any problems?

Anne: Well, yes there are. I'm not sure how to categorize the complaints. I've put complaints about how long we take to answer the phone in one category, and complaints about how long people have to wait in a queue in another. But I'm not sure whether I should put all the complaints about defects in purchased items into one category or into a number of categories. And …

Julie: Oh I don't think you need to worry about that too much at this stage. Just put them all into one category for now. We can always revisit it and divide it up later. You see, all we're trying to do initially is gather some basic data that we can put into bar graphs and Pareto charts. Once we've got the Pareto charts drawn up we can see what causes the most complaints and tackle this. You know, it's generally the case that around 80% of problems come from 20% of causes, or thereabouts. I was amazed when I heard that. Aren't you?

Anne: Well, yes. I suppose I am. But there was something else I wanted to ask you about and I can't remember what it is now.

Julie: Don't worry. You can come back to me later when you've remembered it. Are you clear now about what we're aiming to do?

Anne: Oh yes. Thanks.

_____

_____

_____

_____

_____

_____

There are a number of things you might have noticed just in this very short meeting. First, Julie cut off Anne when she was in the middle of asking her question about the problems she was having with sorting out the data. Second, Julie used the meeting to show off her knowledge and give Anne a lot of information she didn't need at this point. She also used jargon, such as 'bar graphs' and 'Pareto charts' that Anne might not be familiar with. Finally, in asking Anne whether everything was clear, she wasn't really checking that Anne fully understood what she had been told. It would have been far better to ask her to outline what categories she was going to use and so establish straight away whether there were any unanswered questions.

The basic guidelines you can extract from all of this are as follows.

■ Listen carefully to what the other person has to say. Give any questions they have the consideration they deserve, rather than brushing them aside.

■ Stay focused on the reason for the meeting. Do not use it as an opportunity to hold forth and reveal the extent of your expertise on any particular subject.

■ Make what you have to say clear and simple. Avoid any jargon the other person may not be familiar with.

■ Regularly check that the other person is following what you are saying by asking questions that will reveal whether they have understood, rather than just asking them whether they have understood.

And one final point:

■ if anything important was said in the meeting, make a note of it immediately afterwards.

4.1 Non-verbal communication

There are a host of ways in which you can communicate that have nothing to do with the spoken word. You need to bear in mind that your appearance may set the tone for the meeting, while your posture and gestures will affect the way the other person perceives what you are saying.

The significance of your appearance will depend on the circumstances. You may not, for example, have to give as much thought to your appearance for a meeting with a member of your team as for a meeting with a senior manager in your organization or a customer from outside. The cardinal rule is that first impressions are important: if you want to convince someone that you mean business, it is better to be smart and well-groomed rather than untidy, even if informal dress is perfectly acceptable.

Your posture also plays a part in creating a good or bad first impression: standing or sitting upright gives a much more positive image than slumping.

> It is said that your body language can account for over half the impact of your message on the listener.

Your posture is part of what is called your **body language** – that is, the physical signals we give, either consciously or unconsciously, that communicate a message. Such signals can communicate a great deal, so it's obviously vital to be aware of your own as well as being able to read those given by others.

In addition to posture, the signals of body language include gestures and facial expressions.

Activity 3

6 mins

Can you think of a gesture that symbolizes each of the following?

■ Agreement

_____

■ Disagreement

_____

■ Boredom

_____

■ Anger

_____

■ Approval

_____

■ Triumph

_____

Some of these gestures are easier to identify than others. In British society, agreement is shown by nodding the head up and down while disagreement is shown by shaking the head from side to side. (It's exactly the opposite in India, where people shake their heads in agreement.) Boredom is often shown by yawning or supporting your head on your hand. Anger can be demonstrated by a shake of the fist or banging a desk or table. Approval is shown by the thumb-up sign, while triumph is displayed by jabbing the air with a fist.

Of course, the signals of body language are often more subtle than the gestures you listed in Activity 1. Furthermore, they often occur in clusters. To give just one example: you can be sure that someone is listening to you critically if they sit with their head resting on one hand so that the first two or three fingers are bent under the mouth to rest on their chin while the third or fourth finger points upwards on their cheek; they have one arm across the stomach and one leg crossed over the other; their body is slightly turned away from you; they are leaning back in their chair – and so on.

Activity 4 · 6 mins

Imagine you have discovered that a member of your team has made a mistake that will take time and money to put right. You invite him or her to sit down with you in an office to discuss how the mistake came to be made and how it can be avoided in the future.

■ What clusters of signals on their part do you think would reveal that they are nervous and defensive?

_____

■ What body language might you use to make them feel less nervous?

_____

■ What body language on their part would reveal that you have been successful in making them less nervous?

_____

Your answers to these questions will to some extent depend on your own experience. However, it is generally the case that people often show nervousness and defensiveness by folding their arms across their chest, possibly crossing their legs or ankles, leaning back and diverting their gaze.

You can make them feel less nervous by making sure you have not got a hostile expression on your face and by gesturing with open rather than clenched hands.

You will know that you have succeeded in making them less nervous if they are prepared to look at you directly, sit with legs uncrossed and possibly their hands in their lap. We look at this in more detail in Session B.

4.2 Asking questions

Of course, there's more to getting the information you need than just asking questions – you have to ask the right sort of questions. But what exactly is the right sort?

Questions that don't work

Your questions generally need to give the staff member the best opportunity to open up. The following examples don't do this.

Activity 5 · 8 mins

Here are four examples of questions used by managers in meetings with staff. They are all unsatisfactory. Write down beneath each one what you think is wrong with it.

1 'The question I have put to you, formally, you understand, is that I believe that you were involved with Tom N – that's Tom from Packing, isn't it – in some kind of skylarking with cartons on the loading conveyor. Not that we believe you can't ever have a laugh, but surely when safety's involved your common sense should tell you not to do that sort of thing, shouldn't it? And anyway, the rules are quite clear about the conveyors, and yet I'm told you broke them. Well?

_____

_____

2 'So, when they cut back on overtime, I expect you weren't too happy, were you?'

_____

_____

3 'What's the problem exactly? Is it working conditions generally, or is there something specific this time? Hasn't Karen been trying to speed them up again? Don't you think this might be just a smokescreen, something they've cooked up to hide the real issue? Are they serious? Are they just trying to cause trouble/What's really going on?'

_____

_____

4 'I know that before you joined the Customer Relations team you were a sales assistant in the Furniture Department. Did you enjoy the work or not?'

_____

_____

All four questions were bad in at least one way.

1 This question is **long-winded** and **confusing**. The manager posing the question seems to be giving some sort of 'pep-talk' rather than seeking information. What actually is the question here?

It would be better to ask simply: 'I am told that you and Tom N broke safety regulations on the loading conveyors, fooling about apparently. What is your version of what happened?

2 This is a **leading** question. It is bad because it leads the member of staff to give the answer the manager seems to expect – in this case 'No, I wasn't.' It is also what is known as a 'closed' question (see question 4). It won't give the manager anything useful.

It would be better to ask the question open and neutrally: 'When they cut back on overtime, what was your reaction?'

3 This is a **multi-question**. It is long and confusing, and actually asks several separate questions. Worse, these are a mixture of 'positive' and 'negative' questions. Which one should the member of staff answer first?

It would be better to ask: 'What exactly is this complaint about?', and then to ask follow-up questions to probe more deeply, like: 'Do you think that something else might lie behind this?... 'What exactly?'

4 This is a **closed** question. It invites the member of staff to give a short, factual answer – in this case 'Yes' or 'No'. You may sometimes need to ask a closed question in an interview. But in this case, what the manager really wants to know is what the member of staff liked and disliked about their job in the Furniture Department – and the reasons for it.

It would be better to ask questions like: 'What did you like about being a sales assistant?', and follow up with questions like: 'How did you respond when a customer started to complain about something?' These are open or 'open-ended' questions.

Using open-ended questions

Open-ended questions are questions which get the other person talking because they can't be answered with a short factual answer or a simple 'Yes' or 'No'.

They often begin with words like **how, why, where, who, when, how far, what, in what way.**

Activity 6 · 5 mins

Take the fourth question from the last activity: 'I know that before you joined the Customer Relations team you were a sales assistant in the Furniture Department. Did you enjoy the work or not?'

Write down five open-ended questions you might ask the member of staff instead.

_____

_____

_____

_____

_____

There are all sorts of things you could ask. They include the possible questions listed on page 87.

The most useful way for a manager to run a meeting with a member of staff, is to ask open-ended questions. This gets them talking, instead of just making 'yes' or 'no' answers. Of course, you may then find that you need to ask further questions, prompting and probing to find out more.

Prompting and probing

Prompting questions, such as those that follow, simply encourage the speaker to continue.

- 'And then what happened?'
- 'So what did you do next?'
- 'Was that how it ended?'

If you want to know more about something, you can ask a probing question. This will focus the speaker, as in the following examples.

- 'You say you got involved in an argument with a difficult customer. What did the customer say to start the argument?'
- 'What did you say in reply to the customer?'
- 'How did the argument end?'

It's not enough just to *ask* questions. Whether your questions are closed or open, probing or prompting, they will count for little if you don't *listen* to the replies carefully.

4.3 Effective listening

If, as a manager, you consistently fail to listen effectively to your staff, you will run the risk of losing touch with what is happening. Staff will become reluctant to talk to you, and there may well be a corresponding drop in staff motivation and morale. Listening is a very important skill.

How often have you been in a situation where it's clear that the other person is not listening properly? What, are the give-away signs?

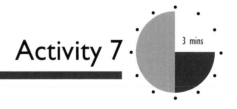

Activity 7 · 3 mins

Write down four ways in which people make it obvious they are not listening properly to what someone is saying.

_____

_____

_____

_____

Among the most obvious signs that someone is not listening properly are:

- they are constantly looking around, rather than at, you;
- they interrupt when you are in the middle of a sentence;
- they ask a question that is irrelevant or to which you have already provided the answer;
- they suddenly change the subject.

Whatever they do, the effect on the speaker is to make him or her feel irritated, frustrated or even humiliated at the thought that they might be considered too boring to listen to.

Probing questions can result in more information or clarify a particular point, but you can learn even more by listening to the feelings behind the words. Is the speaker embarrassed, nervous, proud, angry or whatever? What does their tone of voice tell you? The same words can mean something quite different depending on the tone of voice. Body language also gives you extra clues about what a person actually means (we looked at body language on page 6).

A useful way of making sure you have understood the message a person is trying to convey, is to summarize what has been said every so often during the meeting. You can begin with 'so what you're saying is...' If the person agrees at the end of what you say, you can be reasonably sure you have understood correctly. You can then move the conversation on by asking another question.

4.4 Ending a meeting

It is important to end a meeting well, so that you both feel you have made the contributions you wanted, and that they have been heard and understood. You can use the summarizing technique to check that you have listened properly to what has been said and that the other person agrees with your understanding of what has been said. It is a lot easier to give this summary if you have taken good notes.

5 Formal meetings with staff

Among the formal meetings you can hold with staff are:

- counselling interviews;
- disciplinary interviews;
- first-stage grievance interviews;
- weekly, fortnightly or monthly progress meetings;
- appraisal meetings.

Activity 8 · 2 mins

What would you say is the main task of the manager in the majority of formal one-to-one meetings with staff? Tick the box which best sums it up.

- To give the staff member information. ☐
- To get a relaxed and informal conversation going. ☐
- To give the staff member the opportunity to ask questions. ☐
- To get useful information out of the staff member. ☐

In fact, the most significant element of all formal meetings with staff is getting staff to talk and provide information.

- In counselling interviews: about their worries and problems.
- In disciplinary interviews: about their version of events, their explanation and attitude.
- In grievance interviews: about the nature and origins of their grievance, and what they want to happen as a result.
- In progress meetings: about what they have and haven't managed to achieve and any problems they may be encountering.
- In appraisal meetings: about their progress in achieving their performance objectives and their understanding of their strengths and weaknesses, successes and failures, and training needs.

The important thing is to get the staff member speaking rather than doing too much speaking yourself. The questioning techniques we have already covered are vital for a successful meeting. There is more about interviewing in Session C.

■ 6 Taking notes

In a formal meeting, it is vital that you make notes on your conversation and its outcomes. Whenever possible, prepare a list of questions in advance, and then:

- write brief notes and comments against each question as you go along;
- as soon as the meeting has finished, go back over your notes and expand them or correct them while your memory is still fresh.

Note-taking is a skill that requires practice. It's always a mistake to try and write down everything the other person says in a meeting. Far better is to listen and then write down the main points in your own words, using headings and numbers wherever possible.

Remember to always treat any notes you take in a formal one-to-one meeting as confidential.

Activity 9 · 30 mins

For this Activity you need to identify one formal meeting with a member of staff that has already taken place, and one that you know will take place very shortly.

1   Thinking about the meeting that has already taken place, write a brief account of the following.

■ The preparations you made for the meeting (such as booking an appropriate room and drawing up a list of questions).
■ What was discussed during the meeting (do you have sufficient notes on this?).
■ How the meeting was concluded (again, are your notes sufficient?).

_____

_____

_____

_____

_____

_____

In writing this account, what have you learnt about your skills in framing questions and taking notes? In what ways can they be improved?

_____

_____

_____

2   Thinking about the future meeting, write a brief account of the following (before and after the meeting, as appropriate).

- The preparations you make for the meeting (including your list of questions).
- The answers you receive to your original questions.
- The answers you receive to any follow-up probing questions.
- How the meeting is concluded.

_____

_____

_____

_____

_____

When you have written this account, review it and identify any ways in which you think your questioning, listening and note-taking skills may have improved since you completed part I of this Activity.

_____

_____

_____

7 Other methods of one-to-one communication

So far in this session we have concentrated on communication in the form of one-to-one meetings – in particular, one-to-one meetings with staff. In fact, many of the guidelines that apply to meetings with staff also apply to meetings with people in other departments or outside the organization altogether. Whoever the other person is, the meeting will be more productive if you pay attention to their body language and employ your listening and questioning skills to the full. Depending on the precise purpose of the meeting, it may also be helpful to have a list of questions against which you can make notes.

Of course, there are many situations at work where a meeting is not the most appropriate form of communication with another person. A brief conversation, either in person or on the phone, may be all that is required if you want to sort something out quickly or make an arrangement. In different circumstances, you may feel that a written form of communication, such as a letter, fax, memo, or formal report, is more appropriate. Nowadays, a much-favoured form of communication is sending and receiving e-mails. These have the advantage of providing quick and informal communication in the same way as a conversation on the phone, but you can also print them out and keep copies in a file.

Here we are going to look at just some of these alternative methods of communication and how you can employ them to greater effect, concentrating on:

- the phone;
- e-mails;
- letters.

7.1 Using the phone

Most people think that they've got little to learn about using the phone. But in fact, many of us could improve our telephone skills.

Activity 10 · 3 mins

Think of the last two or three times you've been rung up at home by telesales people. What characteristics would you say that they all have in common? Jot down as many as you can think of.

_____

_____

_____

Have you noticed that no matter how rude you are to telesales people, they always manage to remain polite? Some of them also manage to sound friendly. Furthermore, they always know exactly what it is they're going to say, and they always speak slowly and clearly.

This should give you some indication of what to do when you ring someone in another department or outside your organization. It may not always be appropriate to do all, or even some, of the following, but as a general rule:

■ write brief notes on what you're going to say before you pick up the phone (and, where you know it will be important to have a record of the conversation, jot down brief notes on what the other person says as you go along);
■ stay polite throughout the conversation;
■ stay sounding friendly throughout the conversation (keeping a smile on your face will help you to do this);
■ speak slowly and clearly.

7.2 Sending e-mails

E-mails are being used more and more to communicate with others both within and outside the organization. They have the great advantage of being extremely quick to use. However, they can also be completely inappropriate in situations where it's important to treat another person with some sensitivity or see how they react to a particular message.

An over-reliance on e-mail can also result in a number of problems within an organization. It may, for example, become a substitute for face-to-face communication between a manager and his or her staff, with the result that issues that should be discussed are left unresolved. It may also result in people being overwhelmed by the number of messages they receive, as they are endlessly copied in on messages sent between others. This can have unfortunate consequences if it results in someone not reading all the e-mails they receive, or not reading them all properly.

Activity 11 · 3 mins

What measures might you take to help ensure that your e-mails are always read carefully by the people to whom you send them?

_____

_____

_____

_____

The first thing you might do is make a point of only sending e-mails to people, or copying them in on e-mails sent to others, when you really need to – and not because there's just a chance they might be interested. You might also give your messages titles that will mean something to the receiver, and make them as brief, straightforward and direct as possible.

Remember to beware of information overload when using e-mails.

7.3 Writing letters

If you want to get a clear message across to someone outside your organization, there is often no substitute for a well-written letter. There are a few basic rules to follow when writing a business letter.

- Plan what it is you want to say.
- Make the subject of the letter obvious at the start.
- Keep your text as concise as possible.
- Use short sentences and paragraphs.
- Avoid jargon.
- Read through your first draft and be prepared to cut out any superfluous words or sentences.
- Make a final check of the spelling and punctuation.

You will find a more detailed discussion of how to write letters in the workbook in this series entitled *Writing for Business*. The main point to bear in mind here is that while a well-written letter may be a perfectly acceptable alternative to a meeting, you will have no way of knowing what effect it has unless you receive some feedback.

We turn to the subject of feedback in the next session.

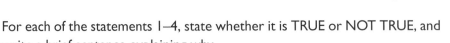

Self-assessment 1

20 mins

For each of the statements 1–4, state whether it is TRUE or NOT TRUE, and write a brief sentence explaining why.

1   If you want to communicate with one member of staff, there is never any more suitable way of doing this than holding a one-to-one meeting.   TRUE/NOT TRUE

2   The great thing about one-to-one meetings is that they
     can be held anywhere.   TRUE/NOT TRUE

     _____

     _____

3   Your posture is part of your body language and can
     have a major effect on the impact of your message.   TRUE/NOT TRUE

     _____

     _____

4   A sure sign that a person is not at all nervous is that
     he or she sits with their arms folded across their chest.   TRUE/NOT TRUE

     _____

     _____

     For question 5, complete the sentences with a suitable word from the follow-
     ing list. Note that one word is used twice.

     REASON   QUESTIONS   JARGON   EXPERTISE

5   In an informal meeting with a member of staff:

     a you should listen carefully to what the other person has to say, and give
        consideration to any _____ they have

     b stay focused on the _____ for the meeting

     c avoid using it to reveal the extent of your _____ on a subject

     d avoid using _____

     e use _____ to check that they are following what you are saying.

6   In what type of meeting should you aim to get each of the following sets of
     information?

     a Information: progress in achieving performance objectives; strengths and
        weaknesses; training needs.

        Type of meeting: _____

     b Information: their version of events; their explanation and attitude.

        Type of meeting: _____

c Information: the nature of their complaint and what they want to happen as a result.

Type of meeting: _____

d Information: their worries and problems.

Type of meeting: _____

7 Which of the following questions are OPEN and which are CLOSED? Put a circle around whichever word is appropriate for each question.

a Have you made progress towards achieving your performance objectives? OPEN/CLOSED

b What happened to make you walk out of the meeting yesterday? OPEN/CLOSED

c Do you like working in this department? OPEN/CLOSED

d How did you feel when the customer started shouting at you yesterday? OPEN/CLOSED

e Would you like to tell me what happened to spark off your argument with Sam yesterday? OPEN/CLOSED

8 What do you think would be the most appropriate form of communication for you to use in each of the following situations? Explain why.

a A member of your staff constantly arrives late and looks tired all the time.

_____

b You need to get some sales figures over to a manager in another building straight away, but the e-mail server has broken down.

_____

c You get a message that an irate customer has been on the phone that morning demanding when she's going to get her insurance cheque.

_____

d Your staff need to be told about a possible change of premises and what the implications of the move might be.

_____

Answers to these questions are on page 84.

8 Summary

■ If you want to deliver a message to someone in an understanding way, and get their reactions and respond accordingly, there's no substitute for a one-to-one meeting.

■ Before you hold a meeting, it's important to think about where it's going to take place and how you are going to set it up.

■ Our body language consists of the physical signals we give, either consciously or subconsciously, that communicate a message.

■ In any one-to-one meeting, it's vital that you listen carefully to what the other person has to say and give any questions they have the proper consideration.

■ Among the signs of a poor listener are that he or she:

   ■ constantly looks around rather than at you;
   ■ interrupts when you are in the middle of a sentence;
   ■ asks irrelevant questions;
   ■ suddenly changes the subject.

■ If anything important is said in a meeting, you must make sure you make a note of it immediately afterwards.

■ The most significant element of all formal one-to-one meetings with staff is getting them to talk and provide information. This means asking open-ended questions.

■ As a general rule, you should leave the job of helping people through serious problems to trained counsellors, but this doesn't mean that you have no counselling role at all.

■ In a counselling interview you can play an important role in identifying when poor performance is caused by an underlying problem that training won't alter or disciplinary action will make worse.

■ Disciplinary interviews should not be about punishing staff but about encouraging them to improve their standards of work when these have fallen below those outlined in their job descriptions.

■ In a grievance interview it is your job to listen carefully to the complaint being made by a member of your staff before it goes any higher up the management hierarchy.

■ In addition to meetings, methods of one-to-one communication include phone conversations, letters, faxes, memos, formal reports and e-mails. You have to decide which of these methods is most appropriate in any situation where you need to communicate.

Session B
Non-verbal communication

1 Introduction

We possess five senses and we receive information by means of all of them. They are:

- hearing;
- sight;
- touch;
- smell;
- taste – which is closely linked to smell.

We get so much workplace information verbally and in writing that we could be forgiven for believing these are the most important channels, but that is not true.

Long before they learned to speak or to write, our ancestors developed ways of communicating through physical signals and signs, as other animals did – and still do. We recognize and respond to those signals instinctively and immediately now in the computer age, just as they did in every age before us.

Conscious language, spoken and written, can convey much subtle and detailed information. But, because it is used consciously, it can just as well be used to conceal what the sender really thinks and feels, rather than to express it.

In fact, if people really said (or wrote) exactly what they felt and thought all the time, the likely result would be conflict, or utter chaos!

Think for a moment. How many times have you concealed your real thoughts and emotions with moderate, inexpressive language?

How would your team react if you always said exactly what you felt about their performance or attitude? And have you sometimes been surprised when they have 'seen through' you, and spotted what was really going on?

What may have spoiled your cover are the unconscious signals that you gave to the receiver, especially in face-to-face situations. Managers need to recognize and control their own body language, and influence the body language of other people, as a key interpersonal skill at work.

2 Understanding different types of body language

EXTENSION I
If you want to find out more about *Body Language at Work*, try this authoritative and reasonably priced book.

'Just look at his body language – there's no chance of winning now.'

How many times have you heard sports commentators say this about tennis players or boxers? Body language is a topic that crops up in many areas of life, but is it just idle chatter, or can you really tell anything from observing the unconscious or conscious behaviour of people?

2.1 The negative …

Activity 12  3 mins

Look at the list of emotional states which follow and suggest how you might recognize them, not from what people **say**, but from how they **behave**:

Fear

_____

Depression

_____

Anger

_____

Disappointment

_____

Boredom

_____

Puzzlement

_____

Your answer may differ somewhat from mine, but I expect it will be pretty similar in most respects.

- **Fear** is indicated by shrinking or cowering away, protecting the face with an arm or even rolling up into a ball as a hedgehog does.

- **Depression** is shown by a bowed head, downcast eyes, a shuffling gait when walking.

- **Anger** is displayed through starting eyes, clenched fists, tightened lips, clenched teeth and heightened colour. Approaching in a menacing fashion or standing over someone.

- **Disappointment** is evidenced through dismal gestures of the hands and arms, shrugging of the shoulders, raising the eyes above, turning away.

- **Boredom** is indicated by yawning, looking about for something more interesting, doodling, clock watching, drumming the fingers – ultimately walking out of the situation.

- **Puzzlement** is shown by puckered brows, facial muscles tightened by the effort to concentrate, shaking of the head; stroking of the chin with the hand.

I've taken more than 100 words to describe those six states, but you would recognize them instantly from observing people exhibiting them.

All these emotions tend to be rather negative, though puzzlement can be a perfectly healthy state when tackling an interesting task.

2.2 ... and the positive

What about more positive emotions, then? Do you need people to describe them to you, or can you recognize them just by looking?

Activity 13 · 3 mins

Look at this list and describe the behaviour you associate with them:

Joy

_____

Success

_____

Achievement

_____

Determination

_____

Enlightenment

_____

Congratulation

_____

Again, you may differ a little from my suggestions, but you will probably agree broadly with them.

■ Even adults may literally 'jump for **joy**', forgetful for a moment of the normal constraints about showing their feelings. Broad smiles, and looking about to find people to include in their happiness, are all the order of the day.

■ **Success** may be shown by a thumbs up sign, raising the arms above the head.

■ **Achievement** may show itself in a nodding of the head ('I've got it!'), or a slight smile.

- **Determination** is shown by jutting out the chin, tightening the facial muscles, fixing the gaze on the object to be achieved.

- **Enlightenment** is indicated by a slow nod of the head, eyes gradually opening more widely, a relaxation of the facial muscles.

- **Congratulation** may include clapping another person on the back, shaking one or more hands warmly or even hugging or kissing the object of congratulation. Self-congratulation might include placing the hands together and shaking them slowly, vigorous nodding of the head ('yes, I've **done** it!').

Detailed surveys have shown that

More than half the communication which a human being receives is by way of body language.

Less than half is through verbal communication.

Notice it took another torrent of words to describe those six more positive emotions – this time more than 150.

2.3 The trouble with words

Former US President Bill Clinton famously answered a difficult question by saying: 'It depends how you define 'is''.

Actually some of the words we defined in the last two activities did not describe precisely the emotional states. You can easily mix up success with achievement, or depression with disappointment.

The positive side is that words can convey so many subtleties of expression and meaning, like the colours on an artist's palette, but the down side is that meanings of words can shade into each other. They end up meaning different things to different people, and so communicate nothing.

Other problems with speech are as follows.

- It takes quite a long time to convey ideas through speech and for the receiver to interpret them.
- Speech does not carry over long distances unless amplified.
- Speech can be distorted or blotted out by background noise, or carried away on the wind.

2.4 Non-verbal communication is simple

Non-verbal communication, whether voluntary or unconscious, is immediate and clear where, in situations of urgency or confusion, speech is too complex. Think of the effect of a hand raised to halt a lorry half a mile away, or a person behind a window gesturing for someone outside to come in quick.

Or is it? Well, usually it is, but there can be room for both misinterpretation and deliberate misleading.

Activity 14

2 mins

Nicholas, a producer of training videos, was asked to show a new induction programme, lasting around 18 minutes, to a director of his client's company. He had never met the person before and after a brief 'hello', they settled down to watch – together with the personnel manager who had actually commissioned the work.

The director watched intently throughout, said nothing but shook his head every so often. Otherwise, his face was without expression, so far as Nicholas could tell.

What do you think the director said when Nicholas asked him what he thought?

_____

_____

_____

I can perfectly understand if you wrote that he said he did not like it, or at least several aspects of it. That was certainly what Nicholas thought at the end of many weeks of work to produce the programme. He felt rather depressed.

What the director actually **said** was:

'That was very good indeed – it does pretty well everything I want it to and we shouldn't need to make any substantial changes. Thank you very much.'

This true story shows that even non-verbal communication isn't wholly straightforward.

The personnel manager explained afterwards that her boss had a nervous tic, an involuntary shake of the head every minute or so – 18 times during the programme. She knew him and so was unconcerned by his mannerism – but perhaps it would have been helpful if she had mentioned it beforehand to Nicholas!

No deception was intended in this example, but I expect you have met the person who wears a cheery smile when greeting you, shakes your hand warmly, then tells you that you have failed an exam, been passed over for promotion or delegated a particularly obnoxious task.

Here, the communicator is trying to convey a feeling of **good news** via the body language while giving you **bad news** verbally. The hope is that you will receive the powerful non-verbal message more clearly than the verbal one which you are not likely to enjoy hearing.

Often, the speaker will then hurry off, before you have had time to resolve the conflicting messages sent.

2.5 Knowing your people

Nicholas couldn't get to know the director who was sending the conflicting signals. That will be the case for many people you meet in the ordinary course of events, like occasional customers.

But it shouldn't be true of your own team, or of other people that you meet regularly, such as colleagues from other departments, regular customers and suppliers.

Observe your regular contacts, and find out their individual traits. This will help you to adjust your approach to them in line with the signals you are receiving.

2.6 Tone of voice – the sound equivalent of body language

Studies of verbal communication have shown that **how** you say something can have more effect on your listener than **what** you say. It has been observed that people respond far more to the **tone** in which something is said than to its actual content. If your tone of voice conflicts with the message delivered, the listener will respond to the tone rather than the words.

'Don't look at me in that tone of voice!'

This is a jocular remark which conveys a number of points about verbal and non-verbal communication.

The **tone of voice** you use conveys far more to your listener than your actual **words**. It is the equivalent of body language, and very important.

Activity 15

2 mins

Look at the following four messages which you might need to deliver to your team. Then choose **one** appropriate tone of voice in which to deliver them from the following list.

Tones to use: persuasive; sombre; upbeat; sad; encouraging; persistent; buoyant; angry; hectoring; downbeat; congratulatory; dismal; welcoming; cheerful; convincing; humble.

The message	The appropriate tone
1 Announcing that a former colleague has died after a long illness.	
2 Seeking sponsorship for a fund raising event which your organization is helping to organize for a local charity.	
3 Reviewing the third set of progressively worse monthly performance figures for your department, two weeks after a new competitor opened premises nearby.	
4 Informing your team that the independent quality audit carried out recently has given your department a percentage score in the upper 90s for compliance with standards.	

My suggested answer is provided on page 66.

You may have chosen tones other than those indicated there, because of differences in how you perceive the meanings of words. One person may choose 'sombre' when another would use 'sad.'

Nevertheless, there are a number of words which would have been inappropriate to any of the messages and would have created an instant barrier between speaker and audience. I'm thinking of: hectoring; dismal; persistent; angry; humble.

As soon as you begin to speak, your audience – whether one person or a hundred – will grasp your tone of voice and respond to it, even before they hear the words you are using. And if they respond badly to the tone, they may hardly hear the words at all. For example:

- if you deliver the bad news about performance in an angry or hectoring tone, the chances are that people will become defensive or resentful and look to divert any blame from themselves – after all, aren't you their leader?
- if you seek support for a charity in a persistent tone, they may respond by thinking of every charity they already support and asking themselves why they should do any more;
- humility has been so overworked by politicians and public figures generally that it almost inevitably sounds insincere;
- a dismal tone may simply depress and detract from (say) the merits and achievements of the person who has died, or it may discourage your team from trying to achieve better performance in a difficult working situation. 'What's the point of trying?' is the message they may receive from a depressing tone of voice.

Swearing, flippancy, sarcasm and jokes

Beware of these.

'Laddish' behaviour, including foul language, sexual innuendo and racist remarks are increasingly cited in Employment Tribunals reviewing cases of constructive dismissal, i.e. where an employee feels that he or she has been driven out of their job by the obnoxious conduct of working colleagues.

Even if the team **swear** among themselves, they may not appreciate it coming from their first line manager – they may find it insulting and patronizing.

Telling **jokes**, or adopting a **flippant** or **sarcastic** tone, can often cause offence and detract from the message being conveyed.

As a general rule, it is wise to steer clear of all such behaviour.

Of course, there can be exceptions to this rule. Occasional touches of humour to lighten the day are well advised, but jokes are best left to professional comedians since many jokes are described as being in bad taste – a reference to another of our senses.

Activity 16

3 mins

Can you think of an example, from your own experience, of a situation in which it is appropriate to use a tone of voice which conflicts with the message which you are delivering? Describe it briefly.

_____

_____

_____

Your answer will depend entirely on your own background and situation. Here are a couple of general examples, both to do with maintaining the morale of any team.

■ You know, as the first line manager, that the situation is grave and can be saved only by extreme effort. You would then be correct to present the facts as they are, but to do so in a defiant, upbeat way. This can imply to your team that there is hope, provided that they are prepared to make the effort required. To sound dismal and defeatist could make the possible calamity into a certainty.

■ If the results are good, but you know they are due more to good fortune than good work (perhaps a competitor was closed for some reason), then you may deliver the good news in a relatively downbeat way, while sticking to the facts as they are. This can prevent the team members from feeling too pleased with themselves, and inspire them to make the next results even better through their own efforts.

3 Sending, receiving and interpreting unspoken messages

Non-verbal communication is a powerful tool – and as a first line manager you want to use it in a positive way.

3.1 Setting an example with behaviour

To a certain extent team members take their cue from their manager.

Activity 17

3 mins

Here are three scenarios. Read them through and circle what you think of the example being set by the team leader.

Scenario	Is the Example ...
1 Magnolia briefed her staff of ten people on wearing shop uniforms at all times as specified, 'even when the weather was hot'. The following week was very hot and she rebuked one staff member for appearing without her hat. Later that day, when she was cashing up after the shop was closed, she was seen by the same member of staff with her hat off and overall undone.	Poor Indifferent Good
2 At a briefing Jonathan stressed to his team the importance of being smart at all times while on duty, and keeping company vehicles 'as smart as you would want your own to be'. The next day, he took a new employee, Ben, to see a customer in his van which was dirty inside and out.	Poor Indifferent Good
3 Gemma was known to be strict about dress and housekeeping in her section, always smart and willing to act herself to clear up stray items of packaging, spillages and general litter. She demanded that her staff do the same. The section had the lowest accident rate on the site.	Poor Indifferent Good

Well I thought that the managers were 'indifferent' or 'poor' in scenario I, 'poor' in scenario 2 and 'good' in scenario 3. Only Gemma was setting a consistently good example; Jonathan was probably setting a consistently bad one.

Gemma's team was following her good example – and there is a good chance that Ben, as a new employee, will follow Jonathan's.

Setting a **good** personal example is one of the most powerful non-verbal signals you can send to your team and more widely through your organization:

'Watch me and do as I do'

whereas the approach of:

'Don't do as I do, do as I tell you'

will fail sooner rather than later.

> In every aspect of life, actions speak louder than words.

3.2 Personal appearance

Two of the examples in Activity 31 refer indirectly to personal appearance, something which sends signals to everyone we meet.

Maybe your team has to conform to certain standards at work which are contentious in an age which favours 'dressing down'. Even here, there is a great deal of difference between being casual and being scruffy, half asleep or downright unhygienic.

> Some police forces are considering a switch back to older-style uniforms. They have found that the newer paramilitary look is intimidating and discourages members of the public from approaching them.

Many organizations require employees to wear uniforms or to conform to set standards of dress in other ways. These will vary according to the job being done and the working environment. What is suitable for someone working in a casino will differ greatly from an employee working in a catering kitchen, a foundry or as a security guard.

Whatever the dress or standard, how it is worn and the general appearance of the wearer sends strong signals to fellow employees, customers and the general public long before they have actually spoken to the person.

The uniform design itself can give off signals. On occasions you have to wonder whether they are the right signals.

Activity 18

3 mins

Both these employees begin work at around 4 am each day. Employee 1, Neil, is a delivery driver for a food distribution firm. Employee 2, Peter, is a postman. They work similar unsociable hours, and both meet both customers and members of the general public as a regular aspect of their job.

Appearance factor	Neil	Peter
Vehicle (exterior)	Clean, washed frequently at base	Clean, washed frequently per standing orders
Vehicle (interior)	Untidy	Clean and tidy
Uniform	Overall, scruffy and stained, carries company logo	Smart shirt, tie and trousers
Shoes	Trainers	Safety footwear, unpolished
Hair	Unkempt	Long, but tied back neatly
Facial appearance	Unshaven, bleary-eyed, teeth in need of attention	Clean-shaven, alert, teeth well cared for
Breath	Questionable	OK
Hands and nails	Vaguely clean, dirty fingernails	Clean and with clean nails

Taking 100% as ideal, how would you rate the messages that Neil and Peter communicate through their personal appearance?

_____

_____

I rated Peter very highly – around 90% based on the factors described. I gave Neil nearer 10%.

Peter is giving a very good general impression of himself and (via his uniform) his organization to everyone he meets, even if he never says anything at all to them.

Neil, who carries his company logo on his overall, is giving quite the opposite impression. He may be a diligent, helpful employee in the way he does his job, but the non-verbal communication which he sends will probably make people highly dubious about the performance standards of a man who is, after all, involved with food distribution. People react differently to the personal appearance of others and the signals which they respond to from associated matters affecting the senses of **scent** and **touch**. The circumstances in which people work also affect what it is reasonable to expect. For example:

- it is unreasonable to expect a mechanic who works in an exhaust centre to have immaculately clean hands at all times;
- someone who works in a smoky atmosphere, like a public house or betting shop, will inevitably have some cigarette smoke odours clinging to them.

Allowing for such occupational factors, there is a whole range of body language which either offends or encourages most people.

Activity 19 · 3 mins

Make a list of the non-verbal factors associated with appearance, scent or touch (for example, nature of handshake):

- which 'turn you off' when meeting other people;
- which encourage you, before anything is actually said.

List as many factors as you can within the time suggested.

Sense	Body language which turns you off	Body language which encourages you
Sight		
Scent		
Touch		

EXTENSION 2
provides a list of body
language factors which
offend or please people
in workplace situations.

Like me, you probably listed more factors under 'Sight' (appearance) than the others, as we take in so much information through our eyes. However, an offensive (to the receiver) odour or over-familiar physical greeting may give much more immediate offence than a day's growth of beard or a creased uniform.

Nevertheless, it is possible to list a range of likes and dislikes that are shared by many people. Such a list is given as Extension 2.

3.3 Managing non-verbal communication

Though taste has not been included in the list there are ways of sending positive signals using this sense. Providing good food as an act of hospitality is a way of saying an unspoken welcome to guests, personal or paying.

Intrinsic factors

Throughout this session, we have concentrated on the aspects of non-verbal communication which can be controlled by their sender and influenced by their manager.

The sender of a message cannot control sheer prejudice by the receiver against someone because of the colour of their hair, skin or eyes, their sex or a disability. Such prejudices, if they are translated into discriminatory employment practices, are illegal in the UK.

Controllable factors ...

However, people of any race may behave in a way which sends the wrong signals to people who are **not** prejudiced, including those of their own race. Many such signals appear in Extension 2. These aspects of behaviour can be **managed** by the individuals and **influenced** by their managers and team leaders towards the standard acceptable to the organization and its customers.

... in yourself and your team members

As first line manager, it is for you to set the standard for your team. Doing so tells them what you expect without the need for any potentially sensitive discussions. Once your team generally accepts the standard you set as their norm, that will exert pressure on any who are falling short of it. They will resent individuals letting the side down and back you directly or indirectly. Where individuals cannot or will not accept your standards and the established norm for their colleagues, then you will need to treat the matter as you would any other aspect of conduct falling short of the standards required, for example poor work performance, lateness for work, absenteeism, and failure to observe safety rules to the letter.

The fact that you and the rest of the team achieve the organization's standard should make it much simpler for you to influence the person whose appearance and/or behaviour is out of line.

Mannerisms and nervous tics

There are sensitive issues involved in these matters. Just as no one can determine the colour of their eyes, nor can they always control nervous tics such as the one described in Activity 14.

Many idiosyncrasies should not offend anyone and some may find them attractive. Again, you need to distinguish between:

- what is just part of the person, such as rapid eye movements or a speech impediment; and
- what is controllable and may be a symptom of something else – boredom, aggression or nervousness – like looking at a watch frequently, pointing or wagging a finger, or a refusal to look a listener in the eye.

You will need to decide, in each case, whether the person concerned is sending unacceptable signals which it is in their power to control. Then you can decide what action, if any, you need to take.

Assertiveness and aggression

In some fields, notably the military and physical contact sports, a greater or lesser degree of **controlled** aggression is essential to achieve success.

Note carefully the word 'controlled'. Randomly aggressive conduct is not acceptable in any sphere – you must direct it at the 'enemy' or the 'other side'.

In most other walks of life, aggressiveness is discouraged but assertiveness is necessary and desirable, certainly in managers whose task is to achieve objectives through their teams – not to do the job for them.

So what is the difference between aggressive behaviour and assertive behaviour?

Activity 20 · 2 mins

Look at the following two situations and decide which is a case of aggressive behaviour and which is a case of assertive behaviour. Underline your choice in each case.

Driver 1, Bill was approaching a roundabout in the inside lane of a busy dual carriageway, wishing to take the right-hand exit. The driver checked the mirror two hundred yards from the roundabout, saw a vehicle in the outside lane approaching rapidly about half a mile back, signalled to turn right and moved out smoothly into the outside lane.

Aggressive/Assertive

Driver 2, Ben, was approaching a roundabout in the inside lane of a dual carriageway saw a queue of vehicles in the inside lane, all evidently wishing to turn right. The driver moved back into the outside lane, drove outside the line of waiting vehicles to the roundabout entrance, then indicated to turn right and accelerated rapidly to reach the circle before the leading vehicle in the queue.

Aggressive/Assertive

I used a motoring example as most readers will surely have experienced aggressive behaviour from other motorists. I would certainly label the first behaviour assertive and the second aggressive.

The difference between them is that:

- assertive behaviour on Bill's part respects the rights of other people, but makes sure that his objectives are achieved;
- aggressive behaviour on Ben's part fails to respect the rights of others or simply doesn't accept that they have any. It is likely to provoke an equal and opposite reaction from the person it is imposed upon.

In most working situations:

- **aggressive behaviour** is undesirable and may lead to serious disciplinary problems;
- **assertive behaviour** is desirable and essential in first line managers and team leaders;
- **weak behaviour** is undesirable and will lead to a failure to meet objectives and satisfy customers, fellow employees and, ultimately, anyone – including the person exhibiting it.

All three kinds of behaviour show up clearly in body language and non-verbal communication.

Activity 21

5 mins

Try to classify each of the following behaviours as assertive, aggressive or weak.

Behaviour	Weak	Assertive	Aggressive
1 Jabbing finger at someone when giving an instruction			
2 Maintaining frequent eye contract during counselling interview			
3 Fiddling with papers and looking down when disciplining employee			
4 Leaning forward and smiling at applicant during a selection interview			
5 Standing over a trainee during an 'on job' training session			
6 Turning away from employee when announcing bad news about a job application			

You probably decided that 1 and 5 were examples of aggressive behaviour; 2 and 4 displayed assertive behaviour; 3 and 6 suggested weak behaviour.

So far as you are able, you need to set a positive, assertive example to your team and all the other people with whom you have dealings through the body language which you exhibit.

A checklist is provided for you as Extension 3 as a reasonable norm of assertive behaviour in business. You should use it to compare with both your own style and with that of members of your team as they behave towards you and their peers.

You can then decide if you need to do anything in terms of self improvement, counselling or more formal training for yourself or members of your team.

4 Attitude, perceptions and cultures

EXTENSION 3
is a checklist for
assertive behaviour in
the workplace.

Many personal, subjective factors are involved in the reactions of people to body language. There are cultural factors too. For example:

- films have been made showing how far Japanese people will go to avoid touching each other, even in the most crowded situations – they become very apparent viewed in slow motion;
- many races are much more demonstrative physically when they meet than are, for example, English people (as a general norm);
- in many countries, people shake hands with everybody in the office before beginning work, which again is not the norm in the UK.

If you work with people from different cultural backgrounds, or work abroad yourself sometimes, you need to be aware of differences that affect how non-verbal communications are interpreted.

One factory surveyed in the south of England revealed more than 20 languages in use other than English. Many of these languages will be associated with cultures which may traditionally view body language differently from each other and from the norm for the UK.

Because of the mix in many workplaces, there can be no hard and fast rules that will work for every situation. But if you get to know your team as individuals, you will discover which aspects of body language in your workplace may be interpreted differently by people from other backgrounds.

The mix in every team is different. If you move from a team where one set of perceptions exists to one where another quite different set has developed, you may need to adjust your own approach to take account of the different environment.

Activity 22

List as many examples of non-verbal communication used in your own organization for the five senses as you can. Here are some ideas:

- sight – including safety or advertising posters and performance graphs;

- sound – **excluding** speech, but including audible signals like vehicle-reversing warning;

- touch – perhaps used in noisy environments;

- smell – warning smells introduced into hazardous chemicals, or appetizing aromas (like roasting coffee) channelled onto pavements to communicate with customers;

- taste – such as samples given to potential customers, or to check the quality of products.

_____

_____

_____

_____

_____

_____

When you have finalized your list, try to think of further uses for powerful non-verbal communication channels which could be used for any purpose. Prepare recommendations accordingly to discuss with your team and your manager.

_____

_____

_____

_____

_____

_____

Self-assessment 2

10 mins

1   The five senses with which we can receive information are hearing, _____, _____, _____, and _____.

2   Which conveys most information to your listener: the words which you say, or the tone of voice which you use?

_____

3   You need to _____ your team members as individuals in order to _____ the non-verbal communication which you _____ from them.

4   The difference between assertive behaviour and aggressive behaviour is that

_____

5   Name two things which you should beware of when speaking to your team, individually or as a group.

_____

6   Give an example of a situation where it is legitimate for your body language to contradict the verbal message which you are giving.

_____

The answers to these questions can be found on page 85.

5 Summary

- We take in information through all five senses.

- Too much emphasis is often placed on the spoken and written word which are relatively new channels of communication.

- Non-verbal communication or body language accounts for more than half of the information which we absorb.

- In spoken communication, the **tone** which you use is many times more important than the **words** which you use. Using the wrong tone can prevent people hearing your words at all.

- **Unconscious** non-verbal communication is swift, powerful and very good at telling us about emotional states like fear, anger, despair and joy.

- **Conscious** spoken or written language can convey more subtle shades of meaning but takes longer to organize, transmit and interpret.

- You need to know your people and their typical body language – and how they will respond to yours.

- Setting a good example in dress, approach to work and the language and tone of voice which you use is the best non-verbal communication you can transmit.

- Team leaders must learn to manage their own body language and be ready to influence their team to meet the organization's standards.

- Assertive behaviour is the normal pattern required of a first line manager. Both aggressive and weak behaviour will lead to problems between the manager and the team and within the team itself.

Session C
Interviewing

1 Introduction

Most one-to-one communication is relatively informal. It could be a chat in the corridor or in the workplace, or a discussion about what's needed from a task, or perhaps a coaching session. Even if you have arranged to coach someone, the way that you speak to each other will usually be fairly informal. When one-to-one communication takes place as part of a pre-arranged meeting or when it is done formally, it is usually regarded as an interview.

In this final Session we will look at the particular communication skills that are relevant to interviewing, and how the formality of the interview affects how you and the interviewee respond to the messages being communicated. However, we will start by looking at what interviews are, the range of different interviews that can take place and the distinctive qualities that these different interviews can have.

2 What is an 'interview'?

We use the word 'interview' quite freely without always thinking what it really means. What is it that makes normal one-to-one communication turn into an interview?

Most (but not all) interviews are pre-arranged. That means that the interviewer and the interviewee know in advance that the meeting will take place and its purpose. There are occasions when an interview may take place without any pre-agreement or warning, but they are an exception.

An interview implies that one person is leading or controlling the communication process (the interviewer) and the other has to follow his or her lead (the interviewee). In other words, there is an imbalance in the power of the participants, with the interviewer having the greater power. This will obviously affect how each party views the process and interprets the messages being sent.

An interview should take place in private so that others can't overhear what is being said. This is because interviews are often about something important and personal – perhaps selection or promotion, discipline or competence, to find out why someone is leaving a job or to help deal with particular problems.

Of course, not all interviews are purely one-to-one. Selection or promotion interviews, and some disciplinary or grievance interviews, could well involve some panel interviews. However, the principles and practices that we have looked at so far apply just as much, because interviews depend on effective interpersonal communication skills.

Finally, interviews may well have to follow some prescribed procedure. This may be for legal reasons (particularly in relation to employment and anti-discrimination law) or simply to ensure that they are done well to produce the best outcomes.

So, an interview is:

- pre-arranged (except in very special circumstances);
- controlled by the interviewer;
- in private;
- draws on the interpersonal communication skills of the participants;
- may need to adhere to a defined policy and procedure.

This is what makes interviews 'formal'. Informality is all about doing things when the need arises, in public view and hearing, unconstrained by specific procedures. Having said that, most people can distinguish between an 'informal' and a 'formal' interview. How is that possible, if all interviews are 'formal'?

The distinction is usually made where the interview is not governed by a specific policy or procedure. If someone is thinking of applying for a new position elsewhere, a manager may interview the person informally to find out why they are thinking of leaving and try and influence them to stay, or you may want to use the idea of an interview to add weight to a warning to someone about their performance or behaviour, without going as far as a formal verbal warning. The communication style used will tend to be less formal, in the language used, the non-verbal behaviour (such as the interviewer's posture, how her or she sits) and even how you are addressed (as Mr Smith, James or Jimmy). What's more, informal interviews are less controlled by the interviewer, giving the interviewee some influence over the process.

Activity 23

Think about interviews you have been involved in over recent years (as interviewer or interviewee). Were they formal or informal and did they have any of the qualities described above?

Interview	Was the interview formal or informal	Was it pre-arranged?	Was the communication style formal or informal?	Was the interview in private?	Did the interview appear to adhere to a policy or procedure

3 Types of interview

We have mentioned several different types of interview so far – recruitment or promotion, disciplinary or competence, exit (when someone leaves) or support (when someone has problems).

Activity 24

Can you think of any other types of interview?

_____

_____

_____

To some extent the answer to this question depends on where you work. In some organisations interviews may be used with customers, clients or other service users. A housing association may interview prospective tenants to find out what their needs are. A nurse or junior doctor may interview patients and their relatives to obtain information to inform a diagnosis. A college or university may interview potential students to discover if they are suited to a course being offered, or to help them identify the best course for them. All of these will tend to be fairly formal, to ensure that they are conducted fairly and effectively.

In the police service, interviews with victims, witnesses and suspects are very formal, because a failure to adhere to correct procedure may prevent justice being done. Research organisations may undertake very structured interviews as part of their work for clients whilst purchasing staff may interview suppliers as part of their decision-making about sourcing materials or services.

Interviews are also part of appraisal or performance management procedures. Most medium-sized or large organisations have some form of appraisal performance management procedure which involve line managers sitting down with the people they manage to discuss their grievance, their objectives and what needs to happen to enable them to achieve these.

From these examples (and you may have identified others), you can see that interviewing, in one form or another, is a very common communication technique. It can involve:

■ one-to-one communication;
■ one-to-several communication (one interviewer, several interviewees);
■ several-to-one communication (several interviewers, one interviewee);
■ several-to-several communication (several interviewers, several interviewees).

Although this workbook is concerned primarily with the first of these, the other three types of interview involve much the same skills and techniques, so we will include them as well, and identify any specific issues that they raise as we work through the topic.

3.1 Formal interviews

As we have seen, the most formal interviews are those that require interviewers to keep to a specific procedure. Sometimes this is because the interview is governed by legal or regulatory requirements. For example, employment law defines the conditions under which people can be disciplined. Employees subject to disciplinary interviews are entitled to certain rights and failing to grant these rights (such as having a union representative or 'friend' present) may make the process invalid. Recruitment interviews that don't adhere to certain rules may leave an employer open to accusations of bias or discrimination in its decision-making.

Diagnostic and research interviews are frequently controlled by written schedules (like questionnaires) that identify the questions to be asked or the topics to be discussed, using both closed (with a limited choice of answers) and open (the interviewees choose their own answers) questions. These are designed to ensure that questioning produces the information needed to enable effective decisions to be made.

Interviewers who have to follow set procedures need to know why they must do so.

Activity 25 · 4 mins

Why do you think that is?

_____

_____

_____

The most formal interviews make people feel uneasy; they are not a natural way to communicate with people. As you have learnt in this workbook, effective communication involves building a rapport between people, but formality discourages rapport, especially when there are two or more interviewers. If the interviewee doesn't understand the reasons for the formality then rapport is difficult, so an interviewer should explain why it is being done as it is. This can help build a rapport. Of course, if interviewers don't know why the procedures need to be followed then they can build a rapport by disparaging them, but this could mean that the results of the interview are less valuable or invalid.

What's more, if you understand the need for the procedures you are more likely to follow them accurately and not make mistakes. You may not agree with all aspects of the procedure but understanding why it is there can help you to accept it.

You should also recognize that the formality makes interviewees (and interviewers too!) feel anxious and, in the worst cases, something close to panic. There are two main reasons for this. The first is that effective one-to-one communication requires trust, a sense that both parties are being straightforward and honest. This is best done by regular eye contact, smiling, relaxed postures, all the things you have been learning about in this workbook. But formal interviews often prevent constant eye-contact (interviewers are reading questions, writing answers), are serious (because formality is all about being serious) and rigid (people are on edge and not relaxed).

The second reason is that formal interviews, controlled by procedures, often have important consequences. An innocent person being interviewed by the police often feels guilty. A person being appraised knows that their career may be shaped by the outcome. An employee being disciplined may lose his or her job. The more formal an interview, the more it is governed by set procedures, the more significant it is likely to be, and therefore the more anxious people will be.

Effective one-to-one communication relies upon people being relaxed, open and honest. Formal interviews can be a barrier to this. In Section 5 we will look at what you can do to overcome these barriers. However before doing so, we will look in more detail at 3 specific formal interviews that you may have to conduct.

3.5 Informal interviews

Informal interviews, where no specific procedure is being followed, which may have been arranged spontaneously, don't suffer many of the barriers we have looked at. Interviewers and interviewees will be more relaxed, less anxious (although that isn't always true – it can depend on the cause of the interview) and establish a better rapport more quickly.

That doesn't mean that they will be better interviews. They can be unstructured and unfocussed, waste time and not achieve their goals. Although this is also true of many formal interviews, informality can encourage people to stray from the topic, spend too long on less important issues and not enough on what really matters, and relay too much on what can be remembered rather than having the information that really matters.

Why is this? Because formal interviews often have clear procedures, and interviewers and interviewees are more likely to prepare themselves, collect information and focus on the purpose of the interview. In other words, as we learnt above, formality can present a barrier to effective communication, but informality can mean that the interview process is ignored. This is why the next Section looks at this aspect of interviews.

Activity 26

Think about an informal interview that you have conducted or where you have been interviewed, and reflect on these questions:

■ Were you clear before it started as to why it was taking place?
■ Did it keep to the topic?
■ Did it achieve a successful outcome?

7 Counselling interviews

As a manager you will be aware that staff sometimes have problems, either at work or in their personal life, that require you to give sympathy and support. As a general rule, you should leave the job of helping people through serious problems to trained counsellors. However, this doesn't mean that you can never play a role in counselling, as the following example illustrates.

> Jon's work was causing concern to his manager, Didi. He was making mistakes, failing to complete tasks on time, and taking too much time off sick. Didi realized that some change had come over Jon, who had at one time been a good worker. She called him in for a private chat.
>
> 'I wanted to talk to you, Jon, because your work has been below standard lately. That creates problems for you, for me, and for the rest of the team. Things can't go on like this indefinitely, and I'm sure you wouldn't want them to. You seem unhappy in yourself, and I wonder if there's a problem that I could help you deal with. Would you like to tell me about it?'

Poor performance can often be dealt with by either training or disciplinary warnings, but there is often an underlying problem that training won't alter and that disciplinary action will only make worse.

Activity 27

5 mins

From your own experience, jot down four or five possible explanations for someone's work performance starting to deteriorate.

_____

_____

_____

_____

_____

Such a slide in performance is usually due to something outside work itself, such as money troubles, difficulties with relationships, worries about children, or illness/death in the family. There are, however, also some work-related problems, of which the most common are:

■ loss of prestige, perhaps through demotion or a public reprimand;
■ conflict with one's colleagues or manager.

As a manager, you have the responsibility to try to identify the problem and, if it is work-based, to deal with it. Preventing and resolving conflict is an important part of managing the team successfully.

> The subject of counselling in the workplace is addressed in _Coaching and Training your Team_ in this series.

It is not your job to solve personal problems for team members. A counselling interview has two functions. The first is to help you understand the person's difficulties, so that you can make a better decision about how to handle the problem. The second – and more important – is to help the individual clarify his or her problems and start to seek ways of overcoming them.

In a counselling interview it is particularly important to encourage the other person to talk, and largely keep quiet yourself. The key to success is letting the interviewee reach his or her own conclusions.

You should not:

■ jump to conclusions about the nature of the problem;
■ offer advice or opinions.

You should:

■ listen carefully;
■ prompt if necessary;

- ask questions to help clarify the situation;
- take notes – but remember that they must be treated as highly confidential;
- guide the person towards a course of action that may provide a solution.

The solution may be for the person to seek professional advice, perhaps from a trained counsellor, but you cannot make him or her do so. However, you are entitled to draw attention to the effects the problem is having at work, and agree a reasonable timescale for the person to take some steps to deal with it.

3.3 Disciplinary interviews

In some situations where a member of staff's standard of work really begins to deteriorate, it is not counselling that is required but a disciplinary interview. Disciplinary interviews should not be about punishing staff, but about encouraging them to improve their standards of work when they have fallen below those laid out in their job description. In any event, you should always try to deal with any difficulties on an informal basis before embarking on the first stage of a formal disciplinary procedure, which is to give the member of staff a formal oral warning in a meeting.

The following example will give you an idea of what's involved in holding a disciplinary interview.

> Chris worked as a manager in the Investment Department of a large bank. She was always busy and rarely had the time to check and 'authorize' all the transactions carried out by her staff. Consequently, it had been established that the responsibilities of her staff included checking and 'authorizing' each other's work. If this wasn't done and a faulty transaction went through, the bank could lose a lot of money.
>
> Every now and then Chris had a look at the authorized transactions to see that they were in fact being checked properly. After a while she noticed that there were a fair number of mistakes in the transactions supposedly checked by Dave. When she watched him more closely she saw that when he was given something to authorize, he did so straight away without checking it first. She decided that she would try and have an informal chat with him first to see if there were any problems she didn't know about.
>
> During the coffee break Chris took Dave aside and asked if there was any reason why he couldn't spend more time checking his colleagues' transactions. His only reply was that he didn't know what she was talking about – he always checked things properly, although he did it as quickly as possible because as far as he was concerned his own work always took priority.

Chris then had a look at Dave's file in the Human Resources Department and discovered that he had received a formal oral warning in another department for regularly cutting corners on work that wasn't specifically his own. She felt that she had no alternative but to hold a formal disciplinary meeting with Dave. She booked time in a quiet office, where they could meet without interruptions, for the following day, and informed Dave, both orally and then in writing, making it clear that he could have someone with him if he wished.

In preparing for the interview, Chris had another look through Dave's file to check whether there was anything that might explain his behaviour. In fact, there seemed to be very little apart from his general attitude that he always wanted to get out of the office on time and so didn't do anything that he regarded as not strictly necessary. She then drew up a list of questions against which she could make notes as the interview proceeded.

She began the meeting by welcoming Dave into the office and then explaining what the main purpose of the interview was to establish whether any disciplinary action should be taken against him. She then outlined what she had discovered about his lack of thoroughness in checking other people's work.

Dave tried to excuse himself by saying that his own work was enough to keep him busy all day. However, he also acknowledged that all the other staff managed to carry out proper checks. He thought he probably had problems with time management and didn't really argue with what Chris was saying. She stuck to the facts, concentrating on Dave's work rather than making any comment on his character or general attitude. She was determined not to become embroiled in an argument or make Dave feel intimidated. She needed to hear what Dave had to say on the subject and find a way of moving forward.

Finally, Chris and Dave agreed on a plan whereby Dave would undertake to scrutinize each transaction he was asked to check, and then hand it on to Chris. Once she was satisfied that Dave was doing the job properly, she would switch to doing spot checks on his work. Chris then warned Dave that she would be giving him a formal oral warning as the first stage in a disciplinary procedure, against which he had a right of appeal. A note on the warning would be put in his file but would be disregarded after three months if his subsequent performance was satisfactory. Should his performance fail to be satisfactory, he would be given a written warning.

Activity 28

Thinking back over the interview between Chris and Dave, what would you say are the main points to bear in mind when preparing for, and conducting, a disciplinary interview?

_____

_____

_____

_____

_____

In preparing for a disciplinary interview, you need to make sure you have a quiet room where you can meet without interruptions. You must then inform the member of staff about the meeting. It is usually better to do this orally, but you should then send him or her written confirmation, making it clear that you are embarking on the first stage of the disciplinary procedure. Further preparatory work should be checking the staff member's past record and establishing whether there is any likely explanation for the staff member's behaviour. You also need to draw up a basic list of questions.

In conducting the interview you should always remember that the purpose is not to attack the other person and put them on the defensive, but to concentrate on what is wrong with their work and encourage them to talk freely. You need to adopt a constructive attitude so that by the end of the interview you have reached an agreement on the way forward. Finally, you must tell the member of staff that a note on the formal oral warning will be put in their file.

3.4 Grievance interviews

It's always important that your staff feel they can talk to you. This applies as much to raising complaints with you as it does to any other kind of subject or interaction. There's a wide range of issues staff may complain about, including pay; discretionary benefits (such as extended paternity leave); health and safety arrangements; and work procedures and conditions.

It's your job to listen carefully to whatever a member of your staff has to say before matters are taken up at a higher level in the management hierarchy. You also need to guard against taking a defensive position, even if the complaint seems to imply that you are at fault in some way. In all grievance interviews, the basic rule is to gather information and react in a constructive way.

You may find in a grievance interview – and also in a disciplinary or counselling interview – that the member of staff will want to find out where you personally stand, and try to manoeuvre you onto his or her side. Here's just one example of this.

■ 'Do you think it's right that we should give up 20 minutes of our lunch break twice a week?'

To protect your own authority, you need to resist answering 'No', but at the same time avoid setting yourself squarely against the other person. Start by seeking more information in a neutral manner by, for example, throwing the question back.

■ 'Yes, I realize it's an important issue, but what do you think about it?'

or

■ 'Well, you obviously feel strongly about it. What do you think?'

This doesn't mean that you should endlessly avoid giving a straight answer to any question. But sometimes it's wise to keep yourself out of the discussion by asking another question.

Activity 29

Here are three examples of questions asked by a member of staff during a grievance or disciplinary interview, which you, as a manager, might feel you shouldn't answer directly.

Write down what you could say to avoid being drawn into giving your personal opinion, while allowing the other person to express his or her opinions freely.

1 Interviewee: 'Don't you think there'll be trouble if this isn't settled by the end of the week?'

Your response:

_____

_____

2   Interviewee: 'Do you think it's right that the office are on flexible working hours and we're not?'

Your response:

_____

_____

3   Interviewee: 'Don't you think I was within my rights to refuse that instruction?'

Your response:

_____

_____

4 The interview process

We've already identified one of the most important features of effective interviewing – having a clear **purpose**. By this we mean that you and the interviewee both need to know why you are conducting the interview and what you expect to achieve. Read this short case study and see what happens when the purpose isn't clear.

Case study

Carol has been told that there is an opportunity for someone to work in the company's New York office for two months, as part of a development project, and that she should choose a suitable person to do this. The idea is for the person going to the US to learn about the systems and procedures they use and to see if they can be introduced in the UK headquarters, here in Cardiff.

One of Carol's team, Megan, has been working for a few weeks on a project to review current systems as part of an attempt to improve them, and Carol thinks this might be an appropriate opportunity for Megan. Carol has identified her as having potential for future career development and had asked her to take on this project as an opportunity to see how she performs.

Carol sees Megan in the corridor one morning and thinks this might be a good opportunity to interview her and see if she's interested, so she asks her 'Have you got a minute, Megan?' Megan says yes and follows Carol into a small meeting room nearby.

'How's the project going, then?' Carol asks. Megan looks glum. 'Not too well. We've had so much work recently that we've had to cancel two meetings to review what we're currently doing.'

'So you've not really done anything yet?' asks Carol. Megan becomes defensive, 'I wouldn't say that. We have collected lots of feedback from the team on what works and what doesn't and I've analysed that. It's just that we've had difficulty finding the time to review it. We are really busy you know.'

'I know,' says Carol, who is beginning to wonder if Megan is right for the visit to the US office, if she's going to be so aggressive about things. 'It's been suggested that we could look at the US system as that seems to be much more effective.'

'Well, in that case we might as well give up on what we're doing if they are going to change it anyway. It'll give us more time to cope with the workload until they've decided.' Carol is really certain now that suggesting Megan for the US trip would be a big mistake, as she clearly doesn't think it's much of an idea. There's not a lot of value in asking her about the opportunity.

'Yes, perhaps you'd better suspend things for the moment,' says Carol, wondering who else she can suggest.

As she leaves, Megan thinks that it would have been a much better idea for someone from the Cardiff office to go to the US office and find out more about their system. She nearly suggests it but clearly Carol doesn't have any faith in her so she she'd be wasting her breath!

Activity 30

6 mins

Why do you think things went wrong in this short, informal interview? What happened to cause the misunderstandings?

_____

_____

_____

_____

_____

Things went wrong right from the beginning. Carol knew why she wanted to speak to Megan, to discuss the possible placement in the US office. Megan thought the interview was about her progress in the improvement project. Why was there this misunderstanding? Because Carol didn't think to tell Megan why she needed to speak to her. Both thought they knew the purpose of the meeting but they were at cross-purposes!

If Carol has started by saying, 'There's an opportunity to spend some time in the US office studying their systems that may help you in your project. I thought we could discuss it to see if you would be the best person to go,' the discussion would have been very different. Why they were meeting and what they were intending to get out of it would have been clear, right from the start.

But could Megan have gone, even if there was a good case for her to do so? The case study says 'Carol has been told that there is an opportunity for someone to work in the company's New York office for two months, as part of a development project, and that she should choose a suitable person to do this'. It doesn't say whether or not Carol had found out about the details of the opportunity. The second principle of effective interviewing is to **prepare** and do your research beforehand.

Managers conducting formal interviews are more likely to prepare beforehand, but the level of preparation varies enormously.

Activity 31

10 mins

Think about these two (more formal) interviews. What would you want to do to prepare or research beforehand?

a. An interview for a promotion within your team, with a fellow interviewer from the HR Department.

_____

_____

_____

b. An interview with a member of your team who has had several odd days off sick in recent months, usually on Mondays.

_____

_____

_____

Clearly, in preparing for the promotion interview you would need to look at what the job involves (a job description), what sort of person is required to fill it (a person specification) and what the terms and conditions of the job are (pay rates, etc). You may have been involved in drawing up some of these, or else the person from HR should be able to supply them. You should also have read through the application form (if there is one) and the applicant's personnel history.

For the second interview you should gather data about the person's attendance and also of other's in the team. You will look foolish if the person says, 'But Jenny has been off more days than me!' and you don't know if it's true or not. You should also check the organization's policy on sick days, and its disciplinary code. In particular you need to be certain you have prepared a well-researched case to put to the employee.

In both cases your preparations should also include a **plan** for the interview. Planning can mean drawing up a detailed list of topics to be covered or questions to be asked, with follow-up questions dependent on the responses given, with indicative times to ensure that the interview covers everything within the time available. On the other hand, it can simply mean a short list of topics (perhaps not even written down but stored in your memory). The more formal the interview, the more it has to follow a set procedure, the greater the need for careful preparation and planning. (This goes for the interviewees as well. The more important the interview, the greater the need for them to prepare and plan so that the interview can achieve its purpose, and this is only possible if they know why the interview is taking place and what its goals are.)

In particular you should ensure that the interview process is equitable – that it doesn't disadvantage or discriminate against anyone unfairly. Employment law now protects people from discrimination on grounds of their sex, race, disability, religion or belief, sexual orientation or age, unless there are very good reasons for doing so (a genuine occupational qualification). Most people are aware of this legislation, although many interviews are still conducted in ways that could well be illegal.

The problem is that, all too often, questions are asked of one person that aren't asked of others, or assumptions are made about people that are ill-founded. For example, if you need to ask about childcare arrangements, you should ask everyone, not just women (and you should have good reason to ask). Equally, if you want to check if applicants are legally entitled to work in the UK you should ask all new employees to produce a passport or other documents to prove they have the right to work, not just those belonging to ethnic minority groups (there is a list of appropriate documents on the Home Office Immigration and Nationality Directorate website). You should also check that the place the interview is being held in is accessible to someone who is disabled.

But don't just think about the legal requirements. Think about what is ethically right, as well. By ethically right we mean, how can you ensure that interviewees aren't disadvantaged and prevented from showing what they are capable of, or give their side of the story. Interviews aren't interrogations. A good question to ask yourself when you plan an interview is to ask, if I were the interviewee, what would I think of this process? Ethicists talk about the 'golden rule' by which they mean that we should treat others only as we would want to be treated.

If you:

■ have a clear purpose;
■ prepare and research appropriately;
■ plan sensibly;

then you will find that the interview will be most effective.

Activity 32 · 10 mins

Think about an interview that you have been involved in recently and use these three criteria to review its effectiveness:

Did it achieve its goals?

_____

_____

_____

Was it properly prepared and informed?

_____

_____

_____

Did it go to plan?

_____

_____

_____

A final part of any interview process is to make sure that both you and the interviewee learn from the experience. You should review how you conducted the interview and also give the interviewees feedback on their performance, so that they can learn and improve.

Reviewing an interview involves asking four questions:

- Did it achieve its goals?
- Was it properly prepared and informed?
- Did it go to plan?
- Was it fair (or equitable)?

The more formal the interview, the more formal the review. Some organizations require reports on recruitment interviews, so that they can keep the process under review, but even if yours doesn't, a short review at the end of a selection process is always worth doing. If the interview was informal, fairly short, and not really that important, it's still worth thinking 'purposeful, prepared, planned and fair' and ask yourself what you might do better next time.

Feedback is particularly important after selection interviews, to explain to unsuccessful applicants why they failed to be selected. Many interviewees find this difficult, but if you followed the simple rules above it won't be. Ask yourself three of the review questions and use this as the basis for the feedback:

Purpose	What were we trying to do in this interview? If you had a job description and person specification, or some form of tender evaluation, they you can identify how an interview failed to be selected by references to this. Without such a formal set of requirements, you will need to be very clear about how you made your judgements.
Preparation	How well did the interviewees prepare? If they hadn't researched the job or the organization adequately, or thought through their reasons for applying, then this may be something they should be told about.
Equity	How did the failed applicants compare to the successful candidate, in terms of the requirements for the job and performance in the interview? If you can't tell people why they weren't as good as the successful candidate, then you have to ask if your choice was swayed by irrelevant (and possibly discriminatory) features.

You will be better able to review your interview and provide feedback if you have kept a record of it. It is also good practice in selection, grievance and disciplinary interviews. If an interviewee were to challenge any aspect of the process, perhaps to allege that the appointment decision was discriminatory or that a disciplinary interview wasn't conducted fairly, your records of the interview would be important evidence. Records should include:

- Topics or questions that you have planned to ask, plus any follow-up or other questions you asked, and notes of the answers;
- Observations of the interviewees' behaviour that appear to be significant;
- Notes of any questions asked or comments made by the interviewee;
- Your own thoughts and conclusions about the interviewee, and reasons for them;
- Notes of any discussions panel members may have had (if appropriate);
- Final decisions about the interviewee.

These points would apply just as much to a recruitment interview as to a disciplinary interview, a grievance interview to an advisory interview. The degree of detail that you record will differ, because a disciplinary interview may need a record of the exact words an interviewee has used, a selection interview will need detailed but not verbatim records of answers to questions, but an advisory interview may need just enough to remind you of the discussion.

Activity 33 ·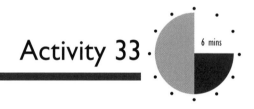

6 mins

Why do you think there would be this difference in the level of detail?

_____

_____

_____

_____

Records of interviews are not kept for bureaucratic reasons – they are there for a purpose. A record of an interview is a reference tool for reminding you what was said and agreed. It is (subjective) evidence of what was said and done, demonstrating that the process was fair and appropriate. And, as we have said, it helps you to review the interview and provide feedback to interviewees.

If there is the slightest prospect that your records would be needed to prove that you had not discriminated against applicants or that you had been fair in a disciplinary interview, then your records will need to be in some detail. If they are being kept for others to refer to at some later date, then they may be brief but clear and well structured. If they are for your own use, to refer to later, then they can be much briefer and simpler. Always think about who is likely to need to refer to your records, and why, and use this to make decisions about your record-keeping.

5 Communication skills in interviews

Interviews require effective one-to-one communication skills, even when you are part of a panel or when you are interviewing more than one person. Interviewing relies on:

- Good questioning skills;
- Good listening skills;
- The ability to build a rapport;
- The ability to read non-verbal signals;
- Confidence in your communication skills.

We will look at each of these in turn, and see how they apply in interviewing.

5.1 Good questioning skills

The purpose of most interviews is to obtain information from the interviewee. That means you need to encourage interviewees to tell you what you want to know without you indicating what you regard as a positive response. In other words, you must avoid leading questions.

Activity 34 · 2 mins

Which of these questions do you think is 'leading' (suggesting what a positive response would be)? Put a tick next to those you think are leading.

Question	✓
1. We are looking for someone with good communication skills. Would you say that you have good communication skills?	
2. What would you say are your strengths and what are your weaknesses in communicating with others?	
3. We like to think that people enjoy working here? Did you find this an enjoyable place to work?	
4. If you were telling people about your time working for the organization, how would you describe it as a place to work?	
5. Peter has told me that you swear a lot in front of customers. You don't, do you?	
6. What do you think customers expect from our staff?	

You probably spotted that the first, third and fifth questions were leading, and that the second, fourth and sixth questions were alternatives that avoided leading interviewees to a specific answer. The questions you ask in interviews should encourage interviewees to describe things in their own way, using their own language and emphasising what is important to them, not what *they* think *you* think is important!

This is why preparation and planning are so important. They allow you time to think about what you want to know and how you can ask questions that will give you meaningful answers. In some instances that might mean preparing your questions in advance, although scripted questions can make communication less effective. In a serious disciplinary case, however, carefully preparing questions beforehand can help you to ensure that you don't make any procedural mistakes that could lead to the wrong outcome.

5.2 Good listening skills

The other side of questioning is listening, and there's no point in getting the questions right if you don't listen to the answers. Listening is not just about using your ears, it's also about using your eyes and, most importantly, your brain. This is what we call active listening, listening to the words people use, watching how they behave as they use them, and thinking about the meaning behind their words.

Activity 35

8 mins

You can't hear the tone of voice or the emphasis with which these words are said, but just by reading them you should be able to identify a meaning that is more than the words themselves may suggest. What do you think the meaning in these answers is?

Q. Did you hit Anil, as he alleges?
A. He was being rude and insulted me.

_____

_____

Q. Have you had experience of working with large business customers?
A. My present company deals mainly with consumers, but some are business customers.

_____

_____

Q. If, as you say, they aren't offering you more money, what's made you choose to leave and take this other job?
A. They offered me the chance to learn new skills and develop my career.

_____

_____

The simple meaning behind the first answer is 'yes'! By trying to present a good reason for his or her behaviour, the interviewee is justifying but not denying it. The second answer is much the same, but is saying 'no'. However, the interviewee is trying to suggest that some of his or her experience may be transferable. A good interviewer would explore this further by asking something like: 'Were these mainly small businesses? In what ways do you think this experience is transferable to larger businesses? What are the differences between larger and smaller businesses in this respect?'

Although this starts as a leading question, it encourages the interviewee to demonstrate how what has been learnt in the present job could be useful, and also to show how much he or she has thought about this issue.

The third interviewee is saying something very important – 'I don't see any real future for myself in this organization'. To move sideways (financially at least) suggests that the opportunities in his or her present job looked so bleak that moving to a new job without any increase in pay was worth doing. If this was someone whom the manager valued and saw as having real potential, it would be even more worrying.

Interviewing is rarely about completing questionnaires, although some organisation's interview procedures can seem to suggest that it is. Interviewing is a management function that provides the information needed for significant decisions and the best information for decisions is rich (full of detail), diverse (concerned with a range of different issues) and, because of this richness and diversity, often contradictory. That's why management is difficult.

5.3 The ability to build a rapport

Rapport means that both interviewers and interviewees are communicating effectively, with mutual understanding of both the questions being asked and the answers being given. It suggests that there is trust between the parties and a general agreement. Rapport is shown by a relaxed atmosphere, an absence of tension in the relationship between both, and by good humour.

It is also shown physically in their posture (how people sit or stand, the position of arms and legs, a tendency to lean towards each other) and their proximity (how close they are). One of the reasons people lean towards each other reflects a tendency to be physically closer if they have a rapport, because they feel psychologically closer.

One other characteristic of rapport is a tendency towards 'mirroring'. Mirroring means that people have adopted physical postures that are mirror images of each other. This is an unconscious behaviour that results from a good rapport having been achieved, rather than a cause of it.

Of course, you may not always want to establish a rapport. If you are disciplining someone then you are not expecting to establish a positive relationship. However, if you are trying to find out about a situation which may possibly lead to disciplinary proceedings being brought, then establishing a rapport by showing that you understand what interviewees say and respect their point of view, can help you to find out more than you might otherwise do.

Note that we have said 'respect their point of view' not sympathize with their point of view. There is a significant difference between these two. Respect for someone's point of view means treating it seriously, avoiding making value judgements (as to whether they are right or wrong) and emphasizing that you accept that their perceptions are honestly felt. When giving feedback to someone you may want to indicate that because you listened to their views, you didn't necessarily agree with them.

5.4 The ability to read non-verbal signals

You learnt about non-verbal communication in Session B, so there's no need to go through this in detail. However, there are a couple of additional aspects of non-verbal communication that are particularly relevant in interviews, proximity (how near or far people are) and posture (how they stand or sit and hold their bodies).

Proximity is about how near or far people are from each other when communicating. Anthropologist Edward Hall, in his books The *Silent Language* (1959) and *The Hidden Dimension* (1966) identified four significant bodily spaces, which for Americans are:

- intimate (0 to 18 inches);
- personal (1.5 to 4 feet);
- social (4 to 10 feet);
- public (10 feet and beyond).

Hall also suggested that different cultures set different norms for closeness so that standing too close or too far away can lead to misunderstandings. In Europe, these distances tend to be less, and in the Middle East, much less, so that an American's personal space is still within a European's social space.

In an interview, when the interviewer and the interviewee are sitting facing each other, especially if there is a table or desk between them, they are likely to be at least four feet apart, a social distance. However, in large rooms and with panel interviews, the distance could grow to be near to the public space.

Why is this important? Because relationships (and therefore the ability to establish a rapport) and their effect on our understanding is affected by these perceptions of space. If you were disciplining someone you would probably want to ensure that you kept to social space and would hold yourself erect and formal. In an interview with someone having personal difficulties and wanting support and advice, you would probably reduce the distance between you and sit in a way that showed concern, being in each other's personal space.

Simply by leaning forward (changing your posture) you reduce distance, perhaps moving from a social to a personal space. However, the place where you interview someone and the type of furniture may force you into positions that you would not choose and may affect the way that you and the interviewee respond to each other.

Activity 36

Think about the rooms or spaces that you would use for interviews. How do they affect the proximity and posture of the interviewers and the interviewees? Are they flexible enough to enable you to alter the distance between them both, and to adopt an appropriate posture?

5.5 Confidence in your communication skills

As we have said, an interviewer should be in control of an interview, and that is more likely if you are confident of your ability to ask questions and listen to the answers. This workbook has been all about developing the skills you need, so completing it should help you to develop the confidence you need.

Self-assessment 3

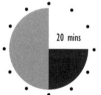

1   What are the five main characteristics of an interview?

    1 _____

    2 _____

    3 _____

    4 _____

    5 _____

2   List three different types of interview that you might conduct.

    1 _____

    2 _____

    3 _____

3 What are the four main characteristics of an effective interview process?

1 _____

2 _____

3 _____

4 _____

4 What are the main aspects of an interview that should be recorded?

1 _____

2 _____

3 _____

4 _____

5 _____

6 _____

5 What communication skills does an interviewer need?

1 _____

2 _____

3 _____

4 _____

5 _____

6 Which of the following statements are good advice about how to conduct a counselling interview and which are not? What is wrong with the statements that you think are not good advice?

a Listen carefully.
b Don't ask prompting questions.
c Offer advice.
d Take notes.
e Draw attention to the effect the person's problems are having at work.
f Tell the person that he or she must see a trained counsellor.

_____

_____

_____

_____

7   Which of the following statements about the purpose – or purposes – of a disciplinary interview is/are correct?

The purpose(s) of a disciplinary interview is/are to:

a   Warn staff that they are about to be punished for work below acceptable standards.   ☐

b   Inform staff that they are going to receive a written warning about the need to improve their work.   ☐

c   Encourage staff to improve their work when it has fallen below acceptable standards.   ☐

d   Establish whether any disciplinary action should be taken.   ☐

Answers to these questions can be found on page 85.

6 Summary

- Interviews are (except in very special circumstances) pre-arranged meetings, controlled by the interviewer, held in private, drawing on the interpersonal communication skills of the participants and may need to adhere to a defined policy and procedure.

- Interviews can be formal or informal, depending on how much they must adhere to a set policy or procedure.

- Although interviewing needs good one-to-one communication skills, sometimes there are panels of interviewers or groups of interviewees.

- Effective interviews have a clear purpose, are prepared or researched, planned and undertaken fairly.

- Reviewing an interview means asking:

  - Did it achieve its goals?
  - Was it properly prepared and informed?
  - Did it go to plan?
  - Was it fair (or equitable)?

- Interviewing relies on:

  - Good questioning skills;
  - Good listening skills;
  - The ability to build a rapport;
  - The ability to read non-verbal signals;
  - Confidence in your communication skills.

Performance checks

▪ | Quick quiz

Write down your answer in the space below to the following questions on *Communicating One-to-One at Work.*

Question 1   What tells us whether a communication has been successful?

_____

Question 2   List **three** kinds of questions that are generally not useful in interviews or one-to-one meetings.

_____

_____

_____

Question 3   Why are open-ended questions so important in an interview or one-to-one meeting?

_____

Question 4   In which of the following types of interview/one-to-one meeting should the interviewer take notes:

a counselling;   ❐
b disciplinary;   ❐
c grievance;   ❐
d appraisal?   ❐

_____

Question 5   Which of these can be objectives of a counselling interview?

a To make a decision about the person's future.   ❒
b To offer the person advice.   ❒
c To help the person recognize the nature of his or her problems.   ❒
d To help him or her find a way of dealing with these problems.   ❒

Question 6   What is the main purpose of a disciplinary interview?

_____

_____

Question 7   What percentage of information do human beings receive through observing the body language of others? Circle your answer:

45%   55%   65%   75%

Question 8   When conveying information to your audience your tone of voice conveys _____%, your words convey_____%.

Question 9   Give two examples each of:

■ assertive body language
■ weak body language
■ aggressive body language

Question 10   Complete the following sentence:

'Don't do as I do, do as I tell you' is a very ineffective way of managing a team because

_____

_____

Question 11   Who has more power in an interview, the interviewer or the interviewee?

_____

Question 12   Which type of interview is likely to be more formal, an advisory interview for an employee with personal problems or a disciplinary interview?

_____

Question 13   Complete the following sentence by filling in the missing words:

An effective interview process is one that has a clear _____, is prepared and _____ appropriately, sensibly _____ and carried out _____.

Question 14   An interview should be recorded to help you review its effectiveness and give feedback to interviewees. Name any three aspects that should be recorded:

1 _____

2 _____

3 _____

Question 15   Rapport means:

_____

_____

Answers to these questions can be found on pages 87–88.

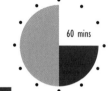

2 Workbook assessment

Please read through the following case study and then tackle the assignment which follows it, writing your suggestions on a separate sheet of paper.

> Terry Newbury had just moved from a department in which she had successfully served for some years, first as an operator and then as a section leader. Now she had the chance to become a first line manager – but she was warned that it would be no 'bed of roses', as morale in her new department was low. The 12 people in it feared their jobs were on the line, as their work could be contracted out to a larger specialist plant a few miles away. Terry's new boss assured her that this wasn't intended to happen, but that unless their performance improved – and they stopped taking time off for no good reason – they might bring about the very result that they feared. A £250,000 investment programme had been put on ice but it could be reinstated swiftly if standards improved.

Terry's predecessor, Harry Mallow, had been known as a strict disciplinarian, with a straight back, jutting chin, fierce gaze and military bearing. He was an expert on the complex plant used, having helped install the machines many years before most of the employees had arrived. He had conducted regular monthly briefings, usually backed by complex technical slides about the machines and slides of detailed performance figures for the past month. Though he finished every session by saying 'Any questions now?', few were ever asked. Harry was always able to fix problems with the machines, in a way which Terry knew she would not be capable of for a long time, if ever. Harry always brought sandwiches for his meal break and never mingled with the operators except on a strictly business basis.

Terry decided to meet everyone on a one-to-one basis first of all, to get to know them. The first she saw, Alf, had been here nearly as long as Harry. He came in and immediately sat in a chair, leaned back with his arms crossed and his legs stuck out in front of him, 'So what's the worst?' he said, without even introducing himself. After all, you know ****** all about the job, so what else can you do? 'Cept sitting in your office reading the bad news old "Happy Harry" used to be so ***** pleased to "share with us", as he called it after the communication course they sent him on.

'And don't tell us again about that quarter of a million they tell us they might spend here, he continued. 'The word on the grapevine is it's only to keep us going till they're ready to close us down. They treat us like donkeys anyway – so which are you, the one with the carrot or the one with the stick?'

- If you were in Terry's situation how would you assess Alf's emotional state?
- What indicators have you drawn on to reach your conclusions?
- What could Terry do and say to gain the trust of someone like Alf and his commitment to the proposed investment scheme.

Draw on your own experience, and on the work you've done throughout this workbook, to provide a skeleton for your plan. You can assume that the investment is a genuine possibility.

Reflect and review

1 Reflect and review

Now that you have completed your work on *Communicating One-to-One at Work*, let us review the workbook objectives.

Our first objective was that:

■ you will be better able to communicate effectively in one-to-one situations using the most appropriate method.

There are many different situations in which a meeting, whether informal or formal, is the best way of communicating with staff. But meetings take time and it's always worth considering whether another form of communication, such as a phone conversation, a memo or e-mail, is more appropriate. Once you've decided that a meeting is required, there are a number of basic skills you always need to employ, such as listening and questioning effectively, reading body language, and taking notes. Particular types of one-to-one meeting have additional requirements. In a counselling interview, for example, you need to be able to demonstrate sympathy and support, while in a disciplinary interview you need to concentrate on being firm while not intimidating the other person. Both types of interview require a degree of sensitivity that you may need to work at developing within yourself.

■ Think about the recent meetings you've had with individual members of staff. Were they all necessary? Would another form of communication have been just as effective? Alternatively, have there been situations where you've used, say, an e-mail or phone conversation to communicate when a meeting would have been more appropriate? Are there any general guidelines you can draw up for yourself on when it is best to have meetings with individuals?

_____

_____

_____

_____

■ Reviewing recent meetings with individual members of staff, what skills do you need to develop to make these meetings more effective in the future?

_____

_____

More than half the information which people receive from you stems from the body language which they perceive, so our next objective was to:

■ understand the power of non-verbal communication and to take it into account when you are both sending and receiving information

If you get it wrong frequently, it will form a major barrier to communication with your team and they may never hear your spoken messages clearly or at all.

■ Are there some ways in which you can improve your communication effectiveness in this area, using both the checklist provided in Extension 3 and the materials from Session B generally to help you?

You might like to enlist the help of a trusted friend and colleague, from work or private life, to obtain a friendly second opinion.

_____

_____

_____

_____

Our final workbook objective was to:

■ recognize and respond to body language and behaviour

You need to interpret accurately the signals which you receive from other people, especially those coming from your own team, and from immediate contacts in your working life.

   ■ List up to three aspects of the behaviour you see which should be addressed, or learned from, to provide an example for you and members of your team.

_____

_____

_____

Our final objective was that:

■ you will be better able to conduct interviews effectively and with confidence.

Managers conduct a range of interviews with the people they manage as well as with customers, service users and others. Most interviews are formal and follow a policy or set procedure but sometimes they can be less formal – it is important to know whether any policy or procedure needs to be followed and to make sure that you conduct the interview appropriately.

   ■ **Find out what policies and procedures you should follow in conducting any formal interviews and ask for help if you aren't sure about any aspects of them.**

2 Action plan

Use this plan to develop for yourself the course of action you want to take. Note in the left-hand column the issues or problems you wish to tackle; then decide what you intend to do and make a note in Column 2.

The resources you need might include time, money, information or materials. You may need to negotiate for some of them, but they could be something that is easily acquired, like half an hour of somebody's time, or a chapter of a book. Put whatever you need in Column 3. No plan means anything without a timescale, so put a realistic target completion date in Column 4.

Finally, describe the outcome you want to achieve as a result of this plan, whether it is for your own benefit or advancement, or a more efficient way of doing things.

Desired outcomes				
1 Issues	2 Action	3 Resources	4 Target completion
Actual outcomes				

3 Extensions

Extension 1

Book	*Body Language at Work*
Author	Adrian Furnham
Edition	
Publisher	CIPD

Extension 2

The following aspects of body language which people frequently find unpleasant or encouraging may well appear in your lists, but they are **not** intended to be comprehensive, and you may have listed other items. However, this list, based on the opinions of large numbers of interviewees, is likely to include many items in common with yours.

Sense	Body Language and Associated Matters which Turn People Off	Body Language which Encourages People to GO to the Next Stage
Sight	■ Untidy clothes ■ Inappropriate dress for situation, e.g. beachwear or shorts in the office ■ Stubble ■ Untidy/unwashed hair ■ Inappropriate make-up ■ Badly worn/untidy uniforms ■ Quirky dress at odds with workplace situation ■ Scowling/seemingly hostile manner ■ Bored manner/yawning ■ Attending to other people, e.g. colleagues, computer screens; radios or TV screens ■ Eating, drinking – or the remains of meals left on view ■ Smoking/dirty ashtrays ■ Slovenly posture/leaning on the counter ■ Turning back on listener ■ Hung-over appearance – head down, shoulders slumped	■ Smart, business like appearance ■ Friendly smile ■ Make-up appropriate to the workplace situation ■ Clean shaven appearance or trimmed beard/moustache, etc. ■ Tidy/clean hair ■ Welcoming attitude ■ Alert, ready-for-business manner ■ Giving undivided attention ■ Looking at you while speaking
Scent	■ Over-strong perfume or after-shave ■ Cigarette smoke ■ Alcohol on breath ■ Strong foodstuffs on breath – garlic, onions ■ Generally unpleasant odour ■ Inappropriate perfume ■ Bad breath	■ Discreet perfume ■ Neutral scent ■ Sweet breath
Touch	■ Flabby handshake ■ Over-firm handshake ■ Touching in any way, e.g. clapping on the back; patting shoulder, overlong handshake ■ Standing over one, invading one's personal space	■ Firm, friendly handshake ■ Respecting customs and cultural norms, e.g. not touching ■ Sympathetic touch in appropriate circumstance ■ Respecting personal space

Extension 3

Checklist for assertive behaviour		
Aspect	**Comment**	**How do I Compare?**
1 Maintain frequent eye contact with your listeners	Both holds their attention and gives you instant feedback on the effectiveness of your communication	
2 Use a range of facial expressions to support your message	A fixed stare conveys aggression. Using a range of expressions suited to the message will help reinforce your message	
3 Maintain an upright, relaxed posture	Whether you are standing or sitting, this will convey alertness and interest in your listeners	
4 Use open, confident gestures	A firm handshake and open gestures with the palms outwards convey sincerity and openness. Folding arms across the chest implies defensiveness and withdrawal	
5 Set a good example at all times	This will assert that you are practising what you preach and will make it hard for your team to go against your requests and instructions	

4 Answers to self-assessment questions

Self-assessment 1 on page 18

1 It is NOT TRUE that if you want to communicate with one member of staff, there is never any more suitable way of doing this than holding a one-to-one meeting.

In some situations it may well be better to use another form of communication, such as a phone conversation or an e-mail. Part of the skill of being an effective communicator is recognizing the most suitable form of communication in any situation.

2 It is NOT TRUE that the great thing about one-to-one meetings is that they can be held anywhere.

You often need to pay great attention to where a one-to-one meeting is to be held. The venue often needs to be quiet and private. You also need to consider whether your own office or a more neutral space is most appropriate.

3 It's TRUE that your posture is part of your body language and can have a major effect on the impact of your message.

Slumping in your chair gives the impression that you're not particularly interested in what's being said; sitting upright gives exactly the opposite message.

4 It's NOT TRUE that a sure sign of a person being not at all nervous is that he or she sits with their arms folded across their chest.

Sitting with your arms folded can, in fact, be a sign of nervousness if it is accompanied by other gestures, such as sitting with legs crossed, leaning back, and diverting one's gaze.

5 In an informal meeting with a member of staff:

a you should listen carefully to what the other person has to say, and give consideration to any QUESTIONS they have;
b stay focused on the REASON for the meeting;
c avoid using it to reveal the extent of your EXPERTISE on a subject;
d avoid using JARGON;
e use QUESTIONS to check that they are following what you are saying.

6 The types of meeting in which you should aim to get each of the stated sets of information are:

a appraisal meeting;
b disciplinary interview;
c grievance interview;
d counselling interview.

7 a 'Have you made progress towards achieving your performance objectives?' is a CLOSED question.

  b 'What happened to make you walk out of the meeting yesterday?' is an OPEN question.

  c 'Do you like working in this department?' is a CLOSED question.

  d 'How did you feel when the customer started shouting at you yesterday?' is an OPEN question.

  e 'Would you like to tell me what happened to spark off your argument with Sam yesterday?' is a CLOSED question, though the person to whom it's addressed could treat it as open.

8 a The member of staff obviously has a problem so an informal one-to-one meeting is needed – possibly a counselling meeting.

  b If the e-mail server has broken down the quickest way to get the sales figures to the manager in another office is by fax.

  c The best way of responding to the irate customer is to make a phone call in which you apologize for the delay and promise prompt action. This will demonstrate your concern more effectively than a letter that will take one or two days to arrive.

  d You need to hold a meeting of all your staff to announce a major upheaval and discuss the possible implications. A letter will not be sufficient as it will not give staff a chance to ask questions and express their concerns.

Self-assessment 2 on page 43

1 The five senses with which we can receive information are hearing, **SIGHT, TOUCH, SMELL** and **TASTE**.

2 The tone of voice is far more communicative – get it wrong and your listeners will hardly listen to the words at all.

3 You need to **KNOW** your team members as individuals in order to **INTERPRET/UNDERSTAND** the non verbal communication which you **RECEIVE** from them.

4 The difference between assertive behaviour and aggressive behaviour is that assertive behaviour respects the rights of other people, but aggressive behaviour ignores or tramples upon them.

5 Any two chosen from: swearing, flippancy, sarcasm, jokes.

6 This would be justifiable when, for example, you need to inspire your team to overcome immediate or longer term difficulties. The facts you have to give them may be unpalatable, but your body language must be positive and confident. If you are downbeat then they will think that you see no way out – so why should they try?

Self-assessment 3 on page 69

1 The five main characteristics of an interview are:
  ■ pre-arranged (except in very special circumstances);
  ■ controlled by the interviewer;
  ■ in private;
  ■ draws on the interpersonal communication skills of the participants;
  ■ may need to adhere to a defined policy and procedure.

2   Three different types of interview that you might conduct could include:
- Selection;
- Disciplinary;
- Grievance;
- Support or counselling;
- Appraisal or performance management;
- Various customer/service user interviews.

3   The four main characteristics of an effective interview process are:
- It has a clear purpose;
- It is prepared and researched appropriately;
- Sensibly planned;
- Fairly carried out.

4   The main aspects of an interview that should be recorded are:
- Topics or questions that you have planned to ask, plus any follow-up or other questions you asked, and notes of the answers;
- Observations of the interviewees' behaviour that appear to be significant;
- Notes of any questions asked or comments made by the interviewee;
- Your own thoughts and conclusions about the interviewee, and reasons for them;
- Notes of any discussions panel members may have had (if appropriate);
- Final decisions about the interviewee.

5   The communication skills an interviewer needs are:
- Good questioning skills;
- Good listening skills;
- The ability to build a rapport;
- The ability to read non-verbal signals;
- Confidence in your communication skills.

6   Options a (listen carefully), d (take notes) and e (draw attention to the effect the person's problems are having at work) are all good advice to offer to someone in a counselling interview. Option b (don't ask prompting questions) is not good as it can be very productive to prompt. Option c (offer advice) is not good as your aim in a counselling interview should be to guide the other person to finding a solution themselves rather than telling them what the solution is. For the same reason, option f (tell the other person he or she must see a trained counsellor) is not good. Seeing a trained counsellor can be a solution – or at least part of one – but it must be something that a person decides to do themselves rather than being told to do.

7   The purposes of a disciplinary interview are as follows.
a To encourage staff to improve their work when it has fallen below acceptable standards;
b To establish whether any disciplinary action should be taken.

5 Answers to activities

Activity 6 on page 10

Among the questions you might ask are the following.

- What did your job as sales assistant consist of?
- What did you like and dislike about the job?
- How did you deal with difficult customers?
- What experience did you gain as a sales assistant that you think is relevant to your work in Customer Relations?
- Why did you decide to leave your job in the Furniture Department?

Activity 15 on page 30

The suggested matches between messages and tones to use are:

1 sad or sombre

2 persuasive or convincing

3 sombre or downbeat

4 buoyant, congratulatory, cheerful or welcoming.

6 Answers to the quick quiz

Answer 1   **Feedback** tells us whether a communication has been successful?

Answer 2   The kinds of questions that are not useful are **leading questions, long-winded and confusing questions**, and **multi-questions**, where several separate questions are strung together. **Closed questions** may or may not be useful, depending on whether the interviewer wants straight factual answers or not.

Answer 3   Open-ended questions (those that begin how, why etc.) are vital for getting the other person to talk openly and explain things more fully.

Answer 4   The interviewer should take accurate notes **in all of them** – that is, counselling, disciplinary, grievance and appraisal interviews.

Answer 5   You should have ticked options (c) and (d). Counselling interviews are not about giving advice (b) or making a decision about the person's future (a), though it is valid to use the interview to obtain information that you may use later in making a decision, for example, whether to offer additional training, or to make the matter a disciplinary issue.

Answer 6   The main purpose of a disciplinary interview is to encourage the member of staff to improve their standards of work when they have fallen below those laid out in their job description. It is not to punish the member of staff, though the interview may end with a formal oral warning.

Answer 7   You should have circled 55%.

Answer 8   Your tone of voice conveys **85**% of the information which your listeners receive and the words **15**%.

Answer 9   **Assertive** body language – maintaining eye contact; open gestures with the hands, friendly smile, firm handshake.
              Weak body language – fiddling with papers or implements, shrinking away, refusal to look at speaker.
              Aggressive body language – staring down; standing over; clenching or banging the fists; pointing or wagging fingers.

Answer 10   'Don't do as I do, do as I tell you' is a very ineffective way of managing a team because your team members will take in far more information from what you do than from what you say.

Answer 11   The interviewer

Answer 12   A disciplinary interview

Answer 13   PURPOSE, RESEARCHED, PLANNED AND FAIRLY

Answer 14   The main aspects of an interview that should be recorded are:
              ■ Topics or questions that you have planned to ask, plus any follow-up or other questions you asked, and notes of the answers;
              ■ Observations of the interviewees' behaviour that appear to be significant;
              ■ Notes of any questions asked or comments made by the interviewee;
              ■ Your own thoughts and conclusions about the interviewee, and reasons for them;
              ■ Notes of any discussions panel members may have had (if appropriate);
              ■ Final decisions about the interviewee.

Answer 15   Rapport means that both interviewers and interviewees are communicating effectively, with mutual understanding of both the questions being asked and the answers being given.

7   Certificate

Completion of this certificate by an authorized person shows that you have worked through all the parts of this workbook and satisfactorily completed the assessments. The certificate provides a record of what you have done that may be used for exemptions or as evidence of prior learning against other nationally certificated qualifications.

superseries

Communicating One-to-One at Work

....

has satisfactorily completed this workbook

Name of signatory ....

Position ....

Signature ....

Date ....

Official stamp

Pergamon
Flexible
Learning

Fifth Edition

superseries

FIFTH EDITION

Workbooks in the series:

Achieving Objectives Through Time Management	978-0-08-046415-2
Building the Team	978-0-08-046412-1
Coaching and Training your Work Team	978-0-08-046418-3
Communicating One-to-One at Work	978-0-08-046438-1
Developing Yourself and Others	978-0-08-046414-5
Effective Meetings for Managers	978-0-08-046439-8
Giving Briefings and Making Presentations in the Workplace	978-0-08-046436-7
Influencing Others at Work	978-0-08-046435-0
Introduction to Leadership	978-0-08-046411-4
Managing Conflict in the Workplace	978-0-08-046416-9
Managing Creativity and Innovation in the Workplace	978-0-08-046441-1
Managing Customer Service	978-0-08-046419-0
Managing Health and Safety at Work	978-0-08-046426-8
Managing Performance	978-0-08-046429-9
Managing Projects	978-0-08-046425-1
Managing Stress in the Workplace	978-0-08-046417-6
Managing the Effective Use of Equipment	978-0-08-046432-9
Managing the Efficient Use of Materials	978-0-08-046431-2
Managing the Employment Relationship	978-0-08-046443-5
Marketing for Managers	978-0-08-046974-4
Motivating to Perform in the Workplace	978-0-08-046413-8
Obtaining Information for Effective Management	978-0-08-046434-3
Organizing and Delegating	978-0-08-046422-0
Planning Change in the Workplace	978-0-08-046444-2
Planning to Work Efficiently	978-0-08-046421-3
Providing Quality to Customers	978-0-08-046420-6
Recruiting, Selecting and Inducting New Staff in the Workplace	978-0-08-046442-8
Solving Problems and Making Decisions	978-0-08-046423-7
Understanding Change in the Workplace	978-0-08-046424-4
Understanding Culture and Ethics in Organizations	978-0-08-046428-2
Understanding Organizations in their Context	978-0-08-046427-5
Understanding the Communication Process in the Workplace	978-0-08-046433-6
Understanding Workplace Information Systems	978-0-08-046440-4
Working with Costs and Budgets	978-0-08-046430-5
Writing for Business	978-0-08-046437-4

For prices and availability please telephone our order helpline
or email

+44 (0) 1865 474010

directorders@elsevier.com